Easy Guide to Sewing Pants

Lynn MacIntyre

The Taunton Press

Cover photo: Scott Phillips

Book publisher: Jim Childs
Acquisitions editor: Jolynn Gower
Publishing coordinator: Sarah Coe
Editors: Carolyn Mandarano, Jennifer Renjilian
Indexer: Harriet Hodges
Designer: Lynne Phillips
Layout artist: Susan Fazekas
Photographer: Susan Kahn, except for pages 9, 23, 35, 79, 91, and 129 by Scott Phillips
Illustrator: Christine Erikson
Typeface: Goudy
Paper: 70-lb. Somerset Matte
Printer: R. R. Donnelley, Willard, Ohio

Taunton
BOOKS & VIDEOS
for fellow enthusiasts

Printed in the United States of America
10 9 8 7 6 5 4 3 2 1

The Taunton Press, Inc., 63 South Main Street,
PO Box 5506, Newtown, CT 06470-5506
e-mail: tp@taunton.com

Library of Congress Cataloging-in-Publication Data

MacIntyre, Lynn.
     Easy guide to sewing pants / Lynn MacIntyre.
        p. cm.—(Sewing companion library)
     Includes index.
     ISBN 1-56158-233-6
     1. Trousers. 2. Tailoring (Women's) 3. Clothing and
dress measurements. I. Title. II. Series.
     TT542.M33 1998
     646.4'33—dc21
                        97-32736
                          CIP

To the more than 5,000 students and clients who have given me the opportunity, challenge, and experience to develop my skills for this book.

To my husband, who now knows more about fitting pants and the female anatomy than any male should ever know, and who has been sworn to secrecy.

To Jolynn Gower, who afforded me this opportunity, and my editors Carolyn Mandarano and Jennifer Renjilian, who I wore out but who asked those questions that kept me grounded, added clarity, and made a book I'm proud of.

And to the "boyz" for their patience, support, and inquisitve nature.

EASY GUIDE TO SEWING PANTS

Chapter 1

*Choosing
Your Pattern*

8

The Basic Types of Pants   10

Basic Patterns   13

Chapter 2

*Choosing
Your Fabric*

22

Fashion Fabric   24

Lining Fabrics   27

Pocket Lining Fabric   28

Other Materials   28

Fabric Yardage   30

Processing Your Fabric   31

Truing the Fabric   32

Chapter 3

*Getting
the Right Fit*

34

Taking and Comparing Measurements   36

Establishing Pattern Reference Points   45

Refining Adjustments   58

Crotch Length Adjustments   71

Truing Your Pattern   73

Fitting the Pattern   75

Chapter 4

Refining the Fit

78

Analyzing the Fit   80

Adding the Third Dimension   82

Your Permanent Pattern   88

Chapter 5

Constructing the Pants

	90
Constructing Fashion Fabric Pants	92
Fitting Your Pants during Construction	93
Layout, Cutting, and Marking	94
Lining Your Pants	98
Pressing	98
Seams and Finishes	100
Creaseline	100
Darts and Pleats	101
Pockets	102
Zippers	104
Finishing the Crotch Seam	114
Attaching the Lining	114
Waistband	118
Closures	123
Hems	125

Chapter 6

Stylizing Your Pattern

	128
Transforming Darts	130
Changing Leg Width	134
Changing Leg Length	138
Raised-Waist Pants	139
Pull-On Pants	141
Waist Finishes	143
Belt Loops	149
Fly-Front Zipper	151
Cuffs	153
Slant-Front Pockets with Optional Tummy-Trim Panel	153
Index	158

Introduction

Today, pants are a staple in every woman's wardrobe. Creating a pair of well-fitting, well-sewn pants in the right style and fabric for yourself can be a difficult and frustrating undertaking.

The purpose of this book is to guide you through successful pattern and fabric choices, measurements, alteration dilemmas, and construction sequence. With this guide you will be able to customize your pants to achieve the best marriage of fashion, fit, and construction finesse, whatever your experience level.

In reflecting over my years of formal training, and experience with over 5,000 individuals, I have come to realize that anyone can learn techniques. The skills with which you develop these techniques and apply them depend on the help and guidance you receive, as well as on practice. The order of importance, as experienced sewers will confirm, places fitting first. After trial and error, and despite a well-chosen pattern and accompanying fabric, many of us, including me, have ended up with a less than desirable end product. Time, money, and effort are wasted, and your frustration level is a 10! We've all been there.

In my early career stages I would sew something and it fit. As I matured and I continued to perfect my techniques and refine my skills, I became more particular about fit as my body was subtly changing. Fitting became more of a challenge and of interest to me. If the fit isn't right, why bother! Few garments require the methodical logic and analytical decision making that pants do. *Easy Guide to Sewing Pants* will help you develop the skills and train you in the techniques so you can achieve better results without the pitfalls.

As a beginner or pants enthusiast, *Easy Guide to Sewing Pants* offers you step-by-step instructions to complete your pants. Whether you use this book sequentially, chapter by chapter, or as a reference if you are an experienced sewer, my intent is to establish successful guidelines for everyone to follow. You can direct your learning by choosing techniques based on what is most appropriate for your personal style and ability, as well as making fitting and alteration decisions.

You will learn:
• How to choose the best style, pattern, fabric, and notions
• What your pattern and guide sheet don't tell you
• How to build and enhance your skills by selecting from a variety of techniques to get the look you want and the "why" behind your choices
• How to enhance your garment with simplified details
• How to personalize your pants with easy pattern changes

Whether you are making jeans, slacks, trousers, or pants for another person in whatever style, good things well done require help, patience, persistence, and practice. If you are an individual sewer or professional dressmaker, *Easy Guide to Sewing Pants* will make this process easier and more fun.

1 *Choosing Your Pattern*

Feeling good can be a direct result of looking good. Few garments are as flattering and comfortable as well-fitting pants. In order to qualify as such, pants must fit to perfection and be flawlessly smooth while you're standing, yet have just the right amount of ease so they are comfortable while you're sitting. And perfect-fitting pants must also allow you to perform all sorts of activities without binding, cutting between the cheeks, riding down in the back, riding up at the ankles, or feeling tight in the waist when you bend over. To top it all off, they must complement your figure!

But fit and comfort are not synonymous. Fit is how your pants look, while comfort is how they feel. When choosing a pants pattern, you should consider the activity for which the pants will be worn. What will be the purpose of these pants? Pants for bike riding will be different than the pants you slip into Monday morning for work. Next, you should consider the style of pants you want. This includes the silhouette—the shape or look pants give your body from a distance (see Figure Silhouettes and Proportions on p. 18)—and structure—the lines within the silhouette formed by the waist treatment, darts, pleats, zipper/closure, gathers, creases, and pockets (see Structural Details on p. 21). Before you can choose a pattern or consider the style of pants you want, though, you need to know differences between the three basic types of pants.

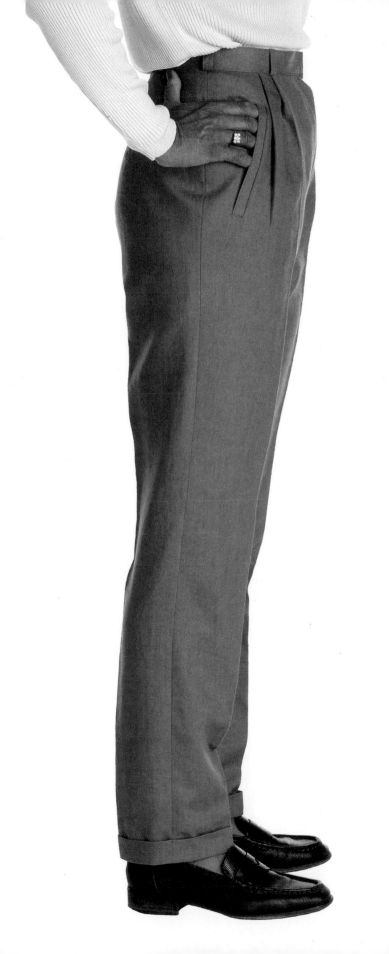

The Basic Types of Pants

The word "pants" is a generic term that refers to three principle categories of fit between the waist and crotch. Jeans, slacks, and trousers—all pants—look and fit differently. Each is designed with varying amounts of ease to specifically accommodate different activities or purposes.

The distinguishing difference between jeans, slacks, and trousers is the length of the crotch extension (see the illustration below), which affects the way the pants fit or conform to the body (see the illustration on the facing page).

Traditional jeans have the shortest crotch extension because they closely contour the body in front and back. Body shape and figure variances are very visible. Jeans are designed for activities with a lot of movement and where a tight fit

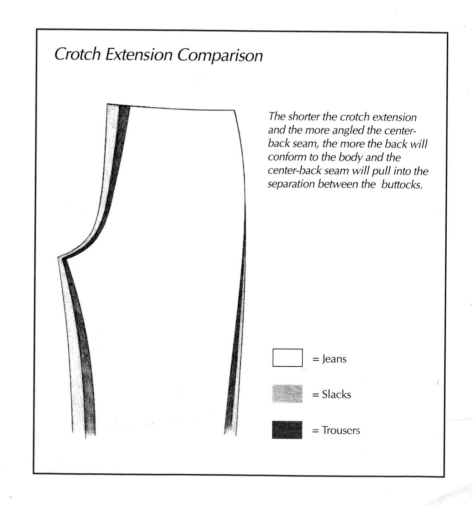

Crotch Extension Comparison

The shorter the crotch extension and the more angled the center-back seam, the more the back will conform to the body and the center-back seam will pull into the separation between the buttocks.

☐ = Jeans

▨ = Slacks

■ = Trousers

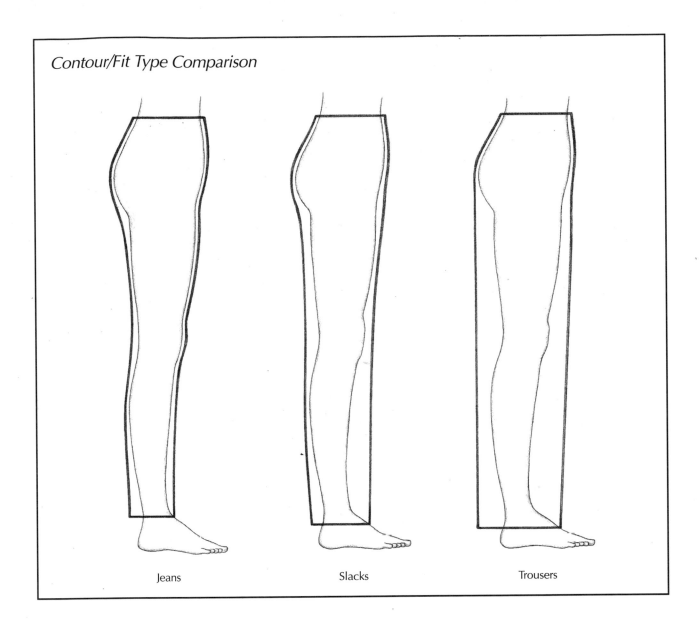

Contour/Fit Type Comparison

Jeans   Slacks   Trousers

is needed. Usually described as close fitting, jeans are a fitting challenge.

Slacks have a crotch extension that is longer than jeans but less than trousers. Slacks slightly contour the tummy and buttocks. Body shape is somewhat visible, and the slacks cup under the buttocks. Many pattern companies use this type of pants for their basic fitting shell because it allows you the flexibility to contour the fit closer to jeans or looser like trousers. Slacks are usually described as fitted or semi-fitted (see the left photo on p. 12).

Slacks are less fitted than jeans but more than trousers. They are a good choice for a basic pattern.

Trousers are the longest in the crotch area and the least fitted, making them particularly easy to sew and wear.

Trousers have the longest crotch extension, conform the least to the contours of the body, and are the easiest pants to fit. They hang straight from the hip. Alterations are usually unnecessary if weight fluctuates slightly. Trousers are usually described as loose to very loose fitting (see the right photo above).

Selecting the correct type of pants pattern (jeans, slacks, trousers) will go a long way toward giving you the silhouette you want, as well as needed comfort. As a rule, the more the pants conform to the body, the harder they are to fit. Because of the basic design differences between the three types of pants, I do not recommend that you take a trousers pattern and try and fit it like jeans, or vice versa. For ease of fitting and sewing, consider choosing a pattern with limited pleats or gathers at the waist and a straight or wide (baggy) leg. Whether you are a beginner or an experienced sewer, this silhouette is complementary to a majority of figure types and is adaptable to all skill

Most pattern companies have basic patterns that will work well for the fitting process. Which pattern you choose is up to you.

levels, depending on the details you select. If you want to concentrate on fit or if pants are going to be a major staple in your wardrobe (meaning that you will be making more than one pair), consider selecting a basic pattern.

Basic Patterns

A basic pattern, also known as a master, sloper, block, or foundation, is a simple, semi-fitted pattern with few sewing details. Usually this is a no-frills slack-type pattern. Because of its simplicity, it is used to refine the fit of pants. Once the fitting process has been refined, you emerge with a customized personal master pattern that you can use over and over. By making simple design changes, you can obtain an unlimited variety of styles and details with the assurance of a good fit. Ready-to-wear (RTW) and pattern companies use basic patterns to develop the stylized garments and patterns you buy.

There are many advantages to using a basic pattern. There is no guessing at ease amounts, and the adjustments are the same for each pair of pants you make for the same fit and pattern company. And you have the flexibility to change the style of your pants without being dependent on commercial patterns, so you'll never be out of fashion.

Most pattern companies offer fitting patterns, which include a pants front, back, and waistband. With some simple changes to a fitting pattern (discussed in Chapter 5), you can do your own creative designing with consistent and predictable results. Once you know what changes you need to make on a specific fitting pattern, those changes will automatically apply to every pattern from the same company. Your basic pattern also enables you to compare ease and fit of similarly styled garments from different pattern companies.

Choosing a basic fitting pattern

If you are an experienced sewer, choose a pattern from the pattern company you normally use. If you've sewn very little, look through the various pattern books and go with the company whose designs appeal to you most. When selecting a pattern, keep it as simple as possible. If no fitting pattern is available, choose a slack-type pants. Details can be added after fitting.

Choose a pattern without pockets. Pants with side inseam pockets are easier to fit than pants with slant or Western-style pockets. This will give you a pattern with a full side front for easier fitting. Two darts or pleats on each side of the front and two darts on each side of the back make it easier to custom fit the pattern.

To determine the skill level needed for your pattern, refer to the terms used by the pattern companies to describe the fitting and sewing levels required to complete the pants. Descriptions of these terms, such as jiffy, beginner's choice, easy, average, and advanced, are found in the back of the pattern book. These are also clues as to the amount of time your pants will take.

Choosing the correct size

A pattern size is only an estimate of what will possibly fit, and pattern companies don't label pattern sizes the same way. So it's important that you always consult the pattern measurement sizing chart (found on the back of the pattern or in the pattern book) for the pattern company you choose. Keep in mind that you're choosing a pattern size based on what goes into the pants, not based on RTW sizes. RTW has no standards for measurement sizing as pattern companies do. For example, my RTW pants range from size 4 to size 10. I measure for a size 14

If you have flat buttocks and/or thin legs, go down one additional pattern size.

pattern, but generally select a size 12. And I select a size 10 if the pants are described as loose or very loose fitting.

When measuring for a pattern size, do so based on your hip measurement. Snugly measure around the *fullest* part of your hip (the average fullest part is between 7 in. and 9 in. below the waist). Fit is affected by what you wear under your pants, so be sure you measure over undergarments and/or pantyhose. If your measurement is between sizes, choose the smaller size, even though you may be closer to the larger one. For example if your hip measurement is 39½ in., choose a size 14 with a 38-in. hip measurement instead of a size 16 with a 40-in. hip measurement.

Although your hip measurement is 39½ in. and you've chosen a size 14, drop down one additional size to a 12 if you have an average figure and are not unusually full in the hips or thighs. This will prevent you from sewing pants with legs that are too full. If you have a flat buttocks, no buttocks, or thin legs, choose another size smaller, or a 10 in this case. This will eliminate the big legs and bagginess under your buttocks.

The paper pattern will measure larger than your measured size. For example, with 39½-in. hips using a size 14 pattern, the actual hip size of the completed garment may be 43½ in. This

information is frequently printed on the pattern. Because woven fabric pants are not meant to be skin tight, extra room needs to be incorporated in the form of ease.

In simple terms, ease is the difference between your body measurements and the finished pants measurement (includes wearing and fashion ease). When related to the pattern, ease is the difference between the size measurements on the back of the pattern envelope and the actual pattern measurements.

There are two types of pattern ease. The first is wearing ease, which allows a bit of additional room so reasonable movement is possible without constriction. Wearing ease is added in the fitting area (waist, hip, and crotch length). This can vary slightly between pattern companies.

The second type of pattern ease is fashion ease (sometimes called style or design ease). The amount of this ease is added to wearing ease and will vary with each pattern. Fashion ease is recognizable by the use of gathers, pleats, or extra fullness such as flare. You certainly don't need to add fashion ease, but you might be bored if all your garments have the same silhouette. Different patterns that are the same size can measure differently because of the design ease that has been added.

Ease is a personal choice and should be determined in the measuring and fitting process.

Reading the pattern envelope

Use the pattern envelope to determine how the garment is supposed to fit. Using this information wisely will result in greater satisfaction with the pattern you choose.

Garment picture and description The garment picture and description illustrate fabric ideas and drape. Sketches and drawings give you a better picture of the complete silhouette, including such design details as pocket styles, waist treatment, type and location of closure, darts or pleats, and how the pants are expected to fit. Terms such as straight, tapered, or flared are used to describe leg style.

Fabrics and notions To achieve the illustrated design, a listing of suitable fabrics, yardage, and notions, such as zippers, buttons, and hooks and eyes, to complete your pants are given.

Width at the lower edge The term "width at the lower edge" is used to describe the circumference of one leg at the hem. Compare the circumference with pants you own and like and choose a pattern with a descriptive style closest to the leg width you like. See the chart on the facing page for different lower edge leg widths.

Finished length The finished length is measured from side waist to finished bottom edge. This can be easily adjusted if it is different than your personal measurement.

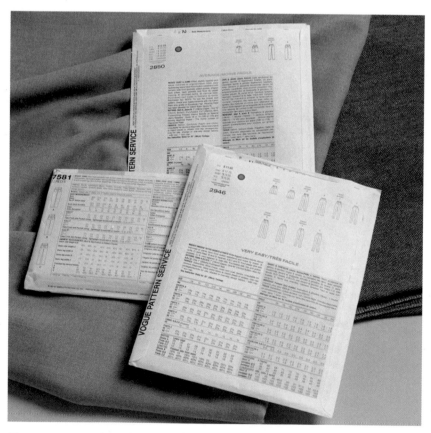

The pattern envelope is covered with information. Studying it carefully will help you to choose a pattern style that suits you, as well as the appropriate fabric and notions.

AVERAGE LEG STYLE WIDTH AT HEMLINE (in inches)

SIZE	6	8	10	12	14	16	18	20	22	24
TAPERED	$13\frac{1}{4}$	$13\frac{1}{4}$	$14\frac{1}{4}$	$14\frac{7}{8}$	$15\frac{7}{8}$	$16\frac{7}{8}$	$17\frac{7}{8}$	$18\frac{7}{8}$	$19\frac{7}{8}$	$20\frac{7}{8}$
SLIGHTLY TAPERED	$15\frac{5}{8}$	$16\frac{1}{4}$	$16\frac{5}{8}$	$17\frac{3}{8}$	$18\frac{3}{8}$	$19\frac{3}{8}$	$20\frac{3}{8}$	$21\frac{3}{8}$	$22\frac{3}{8}$	$23\frac{3}{8}$
STRAIGHT	19	$19\frac{1}{2}$	20	$20\frac{3}{4}$	$21\frac{3}{4}$	$22\frac{3}{4}$	$23\frac{3}{4}$	$24\frac{3}{4}$	$25\frac{3}{4}$	$26\frac{3}{4}$
SLIGHTLY FLARED	$23\frac{1}{2}$	24	$24\frac{1}{2}$	$25\frac{1}{4}$	$26\frac{1}{4}$	$27\frac{1}{4}$	$28\frac{1}{4}$	$29\frac{1}{4}$	$30\frac{1}{4}$	$31\frac{1}{4}$
FLARED	26+	$26\frac{1}{2}$+	27+	$27\frac{3}{4}$+	$28\frac{3}{4}$+	$29\frac{3}{4}$	$30\frac{3}{4}$	$31\frac{3}{4}$	$32\frac{1}{4}$	$33\frac{1}{4}$+

Pant leg styles

Tapered   Straight   Flared

FIGURE SILHOUETTES AND PROPORTIONS

FIGURE SILHOUETTE	OBJECTIVE TO ENHANCE SILHOUETTE	COMPLEMENTARY FIGURE-ENHANCING STYLES	COMPLEMENTARY STRUCTURAL DETAILS (see chart on p. 21)	AVOID
HOURGLASS (curvaceous, small waist, proportionately larger hips)	Minimize curves; elongate body	Straight or tapered; cropped; knickers; harem; trousers	Soft pleats; gathers	Patch pockets; horizontal lines at hip
TRIANGLE (wider or heavier below waist)	Minimize hips and thighs	Trousers; palazzo; harem; straight leg; raised waist; wide leg	Limited pleats or gathers at waist; creases	Over fitting in hip and thigh area; horizontal seams; gathers, pleats, or eye-catching details at hip; closely contoured styles (traditional jeans); excessively full styles

Figure silhouettes

Hourglass   Triangle   Wedge   Rectangle   Thin   Oval

FIGURE SILHOUETTES AND PROPORTIONS *(continued)*

FIGURE SILHOUETTE	OBJECTIVE TO ENHANCE SILHOUETTE	COMPLEMENTARY FIGURE-ENHANCING STYLES	COMPLEMENTARY STRUCTURAL DETAILS	AVOID
WEDGE (narrow waist and hips, slender legs)	Widen hip area	Cropped trousers; pull-on/elastic waist; yoke	Wide or full pleats at waist; gathers	
RECTANGLE (no waist definition)	Create a more slender shape	Straight leg; cropped; hip yoke; trousers; dropped waist; tapered; raised waist	Soft gathers at waist; pleats	Patch pockets at hips; tight waistbands; spreading pleats; front closures; full gathers
THIN (narrow in waist and hips, few curves)	Create more fullness and shape	Flared; palazzo; harem; yoke; draped; wide leg	Patch pockets; horizontal pocket lines; gathers; soft unpressed pleats; cuffs	Tapered, extended vertical lines (creases); vertical welt pockets; excessively long pants; very slim pants
OVAL (full in waist and hips with prominent tummy)	Elongate and slim the body	Raised waist; straight leg; wide leg; tapered; trousers	Limited pleats or gathers at waist; creases; back or side closure; slanted or side-seam pockets; piped waist	Details that draw attention to hip area; spreading pleats; horizontal lines; fly zipper or front closure; excessive fullness or gathers

FIGURE SILHOUETTES AND PROPORTIONS *(continued)*

FIGURE SILHOUETTE	OBJECTIVE TO ENHANCE SILHOUETTE	COMPLEMENTARY FIGURE-ENHANCING STYLES	COMPLEMENTARY STRUCTURAL DETAILS	AVOID
SHORT LEGS	Lengthen lower torso	Palazzo; wide leg; raised waist; tapered; straight leg; flared	Limited pleats, darts, gathers at waist; fly zipper; creases; vertical seaming (princess line)	Horizontal lines; cuffs; hip yokes; patch pockets; flap pockets
LONG LEGS	Shorten lower torso	Yoke; dropped waist	Cuffs; faced waistlines; flap pockets; horizontal yokes	Raised waist; pleats; pants that are too short; creases
EXTRA HEAVY	Lengthen and softly define the body	Trousers; wide leg; tapered; straight leg	Slim sewn-down pleats; creases; narrow or inconspicuous waistband	Too tight a fit; poor fit
SHORT/PETITE	Elongate the body	Jeans; trousers; tapered; straight leg	Vertical lines: pleats; creases; fly zipper; slant pockets; welt pockets	Too much fullness; pants that are too long; cuffs

Pants styles

Trousers   Palazzo   Wide leg   Cropped   Draped   Harem   Tapered   Straight leg/stovepipe   Flared

STRUCTURAL DETAILS

WAIST-TREATMENT OPTIONS	DRAWSTRING OR ELASTICIZED WAIST	FACED WAIST (WAIST EDGE FINISHED)	FITTED WAISTBAND (separate piece usually 1¼ in. wide fitting slightly above natural waist)
	Full; gathered	Raised (above natural waist); yoke (shaped and fitted piece in high hip area); dropped (below natural waist) **Raised waist** **Yoke** **Dropped waist**	Smooth; trousers; jean; dropped; limited pleats or gathers; draped **Smooth** **Trousers** **Jean** **Dropped waist** **Limited pleats or gathers** **Draped**
POCKET OPTIONS Can be decorative or functional; hidden or eye catching; vertical or horizontal. Depending on shape and placement, pockets can have a strong influence on silhouette.	OUTSIDE **Patch pockets**	INSERTED **Side seam** **Slant**	WELT **Welt with flap** **Bound**

2 Choosing Your Fabric

Fabric suitability depends on pattern style and personal silhouette. Weaves and fibers can be mixed together in a mind-boggling number of combinations. In most cases, the wrong fabric rather than poor sewing is responsible for the majority of garment failures.

Your silhouette or visual profile is directly influenced by the characteristics of the fabric you choose. If your goal is to conceal your body contours, look for fabrics that are a medium weight and have a smooth texture and a firm hand. Darker, duller colors visually decrease size and weight. On the other hand, choosing bulky or rough textures, light or bright colors, or shiny fabrics results in visually increasing both size and weight. Soft, stretchy fabrics can be clingy, revealing the contours of the body, or drapable and concealing, depending on the style of pants you've chosen.

When the pants style is created, the designer has specific fabrics in mind that will maintain the style lines of the garment. Every pattern envelope lists suggested fabrics, and although you are not obligated to select one of the recommended fabrics, it is a good starting point. With a basic knowledge of fabric categories, fiber performance, and your personal style (which we discussed in Chapter 1), you will be able to turn beautiful fabric and a great pattern into successful pants.

Fashion Fabric

In addition to style and silhouette, your fashion fabric should blend or act as an accent color or texture and fit in with your current wardrobe. Wear and care should be compatible with your lifestyle and commitment.

Because natural fibers breathe, or allow airflow through the fibers, they are more comfortable to wear in very warm climates. Wool is a natural insulator. Because of its construction, a series of interlocking scales trap air and hold it while the air is warmed by the body. By choosing a fashion fabric with a high percentage of wool, silk, cotton, or linen, you will add to the wearing comfort and enjoyment of your pants. And you will feel more confident in

your pants if you choose a fabric that is consistent with your personal style and image. For example, if you tend to be more conservative and wear classic styles you may not feel comfortable in a flamboyant bright, shiny red print, but better in a muted pumpkin linen.

By following a few simple guidelines your fabric choice will be a success for you and your pants. Look carefully at the pattern envelope for the most suitable fabrics. The first fabric is the best choice based on how the pattern was designed. You can expand your possibilities by choosing fabrics similar to those listed.

Ask yourself if the silhouette pictured calls for fabric that drapes softly, stands away from

Some patterns call for a crisp linen, while others will only be successful in something with drape, and still others require a stretchy knit. Your fabric choice needs to match your pattern.

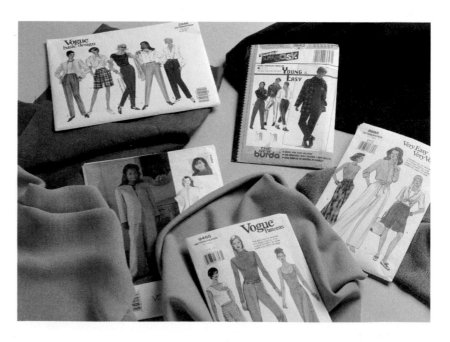

the body, clings closely, or poufs crisply. Your visual interpretation, as well as the list of suggested fabrics, will help you achieve the same silhouette. To do this, whatever fabric you choose must behave in the same way as the suggested fabrics, even if it has a different name or fiber content. Tailored pants styles will usually require crisp fabrics that hold their shape. Fuller styles that may have gathers require a soft fabric with draping qualities.

The following four classifications of fibers are important because they affect the performance, comfort, and care of the fabric. Choosing natural over synthetic fibers is a tradeoff between comfort and care. What you gain in comfort you lose in care.

Fiber types affect how we physically feel in a garment. How we look is equally, if not more, important. How a fabric hangs or drapes on your body can affect your psychological comfort, as well as your silhouette. Poor choices can make your pants uncomfortable to wear and incompatible with your pattern or personal style.

Natural fibers

Natural fibers are those made from animal or vegetable sources. They include wool, silk, cotton, and linen. Fabrics from these fibers are comfortable to wear

Whether you choose a fabric that is natural, man-made, synthetic, or a blend, your choice should be guided by your pattern's suggestions, your sewing skill, and the visual profile you want to create.

because of wicking qualities. Wicking refers to the ability of a fabric to pull moisture away from the body because the fibers can absorb moisture, unlike synthetic fibers. The care of these fibers and their ability to resist wrinkles varies.

Man-made/ transitional fiber

Rayon is a man-made/ transitional fiber because it is composed of cellulosic fibers whose natural source is wood pulp. The fibers are then chemically processed. Although the rayon fiber is not found in nature, it is derived from a natural source, unlike synthetic fibers, which are derived from chemicals like petroleum and then chemically processed.

Synthetic fibers

Synthetic fibers are derived from a chemical source and are chemically processed. These fibers include polyester, nylon, acrylic, and spandex. These fibers are less comfortable to wear than natural fibers because they have no wicking qualities and they are prone to static electricity. However, they are machine washable, resist wrinkling, and hold their shape well.

Fabric blends

Blends combine the best of two or more fibers, resulting in a superior fabric. One such example is a blend of 65% cotton and 35% polyester. The fabric will give you the comfort and wicking qualities of cotton and the wrinkle resistance of polyester. For a fiber to make a significant difference in fabric performance its composition must be 35% to 50% of the fabric. The exception to that rule is spandex. With as little as 3% to 5% of spandex added to a fabric, significant stretch is achieved, particularly in woven fabrics. The look and feel of the woven fabric is maintained, but you get a closer fit with less wrinkling and more comfort. The fabric "gives" and moves with you as you stress it and recovers without bagginess.

General considerations

Crisp fabrics such as linen, denim, chino, gabardine, ultrasuede, silk pongee, and corduroy are well suited to tailored styles such as classic trousers or slacks that require a fabric that holds its shape and incorporates darts, pleats, or tucks. Soft fabrics such as challis, wool or silk jersey, wool crepe, crepe de Chine, and interlock knits drape softly around the body and make up best in fuller styles or in styles with gathers and few structured lines.

Whether you choose a plain or printed fabric will depend on your pattern choice. The style and the fabric should never compete for attention. Internal pattern details such as pockets, topstitching, and pleats show up better in a plain fabric. A printed fabric works best with a very basic style pants with few internal pattern details.

Easy-to-handle fabrics are those that are firmly woven, are of medium weight, have a smooth texture, and are a solid color or have a small all-over design with no matching required. Construction inaccuracies are less prominent.

The most important consideration when choosing fabric, even more important than fiber content, is the "hand." This is a term used to describe the stiffness vs. softness of a fabric. It refers to the drapability of a fabric: how it will hang and move on your body. Choosing a fabric with the wrong hand means the intended silhouette will most likely be wrong also. Fabric hand is determined by the fiber content, construction (type of weave or knit), and finishes.

When reading the list of suggested fabrics, don't interpret a generic fabric suggestion such as gabardine to mean only wool gabardine. Gabardine refers to a specific type of weave or construction used in all gabardines, whether they are wool, silk, cotton, rayon, or a synthetic. It also implies a suggested weight, hand, or drape of the fabric, in this case, gabardine.

Lining Fabrics

A lining is a duplication of your pants without a zipper or waistband. If you choose to line your pants, you will be making two separate garments (except for the zipper and waistband). Lined pants are more durable and more comfortable because slippery, smooth fabrics feel wonderful next to your skin. They wrinkle less, and the lining reduces clinging. A lining can also make a sheer fabric more opaque.

Lining fabrics should be lightweight, smooth, soft, and compatible in care with the fashion fabric. They should also be anti-static, wrinkle resistant, and comfortable to wear.

Lined pants can be more comfortable to wear and feel more luxurious. Choose your lining from rayon, polyester, or silk fabrics. Yardage requirements may be different than for your fashion fabric.

Consider natural or man-made vs. synthetic fabrics, weighing differences in wicking qualities and compatibility with fashion fabric. If possible, choose a lining fabric with similar wicking characteristics as your fashion fabric for added comfort. Firmly woven fabrics with plain or twill weaves wear better. Finally, the color of the lining should coordinate with the color of the fashion fabric. Good lining choices are lightweight rayon, lightweight polyester, and lightweight silk, such as silk crepe de Chine.

Lining fabrics can be difficult to sew because they are thin, slippery, and difficult to control and because it's hard to prevent puckered seams. Additionally, excessive raveling and improper pressing can present problems to a beginner sewer. Try lining the same pair of pants the second time around, after you have learned basic pants-fitting and construction skills.

Pocket Lining Fabric

For soft, slippery, durable, and non-bulky pockets, I prefer a stable warp knit or tricot for the pocket lining. You can certainly use your fashion fabric, lining, or pocketing (a durable material made specifically for this). Regardless of which pocket lining fabric you choose, you should face the pocket opening edges to give the appearance that the whole pocket is made from fashion fabric.

Other Materials

Today there are so many wonderful notions that whatever you need, it's probably available. For every notion there can be several choices. Choosing thread, for example, is no longer a simple matter of color choice. You can choose from silk, silk-finished cotton, cotton polyester, two-ply, three-ply, and top-stitching weights. There are four kinds of zippers, three kinds of tape, and two kinds of coils. So you see it is important to be knowledgeable about what is available, as well as under-standing the type of notion you'll need for your pattern and fabric choice if your project is to be a success. Try different brands of the same product. You may find you like one brand over another. Several times a year, shop the notions department of your favorite fabric store or catalog supplier to see what's new that can make your sewing easier.

Interfacing

A fitted waistband or waist facing retains its shape better if it is interfaced. Interfacing gives it support and stability so it will not collapse, wrinkle, or curl. Interfacing can be fusible or sew in. Both are available in woven and non-woven types. Many

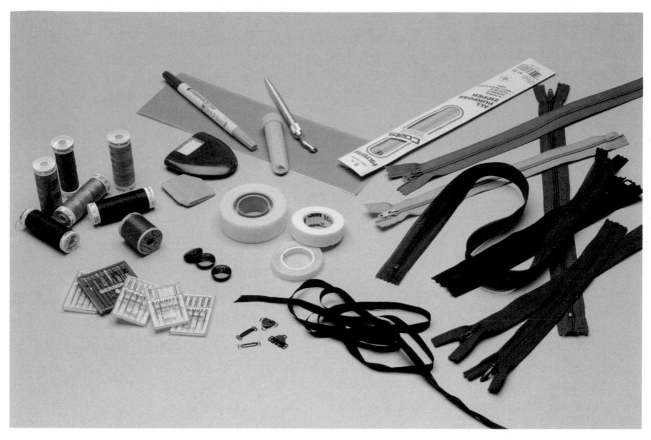

Notions not only include those things listed on your pattern envelope needed to complete your project but also specialty items that can make your sewing easier, faster, and better.

fusibles come in precut widths, with perforated foldlines for easy and accurate application, and can be purchased prepackaged or by the yard. Your choice of waist interfacing will affect the comfort and appearance of your finished waist treatment. For comfort, choose a soft interfacing material, such as a fusible, rather than a stiff interfacing, such as Ban-Rol.

Notions

Consult your pattern envelope for a specific listing of type, number, or sizes of notions. Additional recommendations I suggest that are not found on the envelope are double-sided basting or transparent tape for pinless zipper applications and a polyester zipper longer than requested because it is easier to install and simple to shorten. If using a metal zipper, purchase the size specified on your pattern envelope.

I prefer using cotton-wrapped all-purpose polyester thread on knits, synthetic fabrics, or blends with synthetics. The thread "gives" with knits without seams popping, and its strength is compatible with synthetic fabrics. I use 100% cotton in size

MACHINE NEEDLES AND STITCH LENGTH		
FABRIC WEIGHT	NEEDLE SIZE	STITCH SETTING (in mm stitches per inch—spi)
Lightweight	60/9 to 70/10	1.5mm to 1.7mm/ 15 spi to 18 spi
Medium weight	70/10 to 80/12	2mm to 2.5mm/ 12 spi
Heavyweight	90/14 to 100/16	2.5mm to 3mm/ 10 spi
Very heavy	100/16 to 120/20	3mm to 4mm/6 spi to 8 spi

50 with natural fibers—I have had fabrics rip before the thread breaks using the all-purpose polyester because the thread is stronger than the fiber when stressed. You can restitch the seam, but repairing the fabric is more difficult.

Simple pants take 125 yards to 150 yards of thread, not including seam finishes or topstitching. Choose a shade slightly darker than your fabric. For multicolor fabric, match the dominant color. Thread weight should be compatible with the fabric for pucker-free seams. For microfibers, use a lightweight or fine thread like two-ply 60 weight.

Specialty needles may be available for your machine for specific fabrics such as natural or synthetic leathers and suedes, microfibers, and denim.

Fabric Yardage

Pattern yardage requirements for the view, size, and fabric width are calculations, not estimates, and are figured quite close. Therefore, purchase extra fabric if you anticipate pattern adjustments. Purchase two times the intended length-adjustment amount. Width adjustments may require additional width and length, so purchase yardage for a size three to four times larger than you intend to make or ¼ yard to ⅜ yard more if using

45-in.-wide fabric. You can precisely determine the specific yardage required for your adjusted pants pattern by doing a trial layout and marking off 45-in. and 60-in. widths. Then measure the length each requires.

Natural fibers, particularly loosely woven cottons and knits, can shrink. Allow 4 in. to 5 in. per yard for shrinkage for cotton knits and 2 in. to 3 in. per yard for other knits. In addition, allow for straightening of the grain if the fabric has been cut rather than torn. An extra ¼ yard should be enough to straighten the grain.

If you have decided to line your pants and your pattern does not call for lining, purchase fabric according to the 45-in. width yardage chart, or purchase two lengths (your side measurement from waist to floor) to allow for pattern adjustments.

Processing Your Fabric

Before laying out the pattern, you'll need to pretreat your fabric the same way you intend to care for your pants once they are completed. This is the best way to ensure that your pants will look and fit the same after their first laundering or dry cleaning. Doing this also eliminates future shrinkage and removes temporary finishes or sizing, thus eliminating sewing problems.

To preshrink or pretreat your fabric, check the fabric care label on the bolt if possible when purchasing the fabric and treat as stated. If you're unable to get the care instructions, here are some general guidelines.

Woven cottons should be washed (by hand or machine) and dried (by line or machine). Cotton knits should be washed and dried several times to maximize shrinkage.

For rayons, linens, silks, and blends, wash using a pH-balanced detergent. I have successfully washed all of these fabrics. However, I caution you to use care and always do a 6-in. by 6-in. sample test. If you don't like the way the sample looks after washing, drying, and pressing, or if it has shrunk considerably, *do not* pretreat the fabric that way. Rayon, linen, silk, and delicate synthetic blends are best soaked in tepid water and mild detergent for 15 to 20 minutes, then line-dried.

For dry-cleanable wool, roll a single thickness of the fabric in an evenly damp sheet (see the photo on p. 32). Let it rest until the wool is thoroughly damp. To dry, lay a single thickness of the wool flat. Another option is to

If you don't feel like going to the dry cleaner to preshrink your wool, you can roll it up in a damp sheet instead.

have your dry cleaner professionally steam (no need to clean) your yardage. Do the same for other dry-cleanable fabrics, or thoroughly steam a single thickness of fabric on a flat surface, holding the iron ½ in. above the fabric. Let the fabric rest until it is no longer damp.

Truing the Fabric

Good fit and professional appearance depend on fabric that has been made thread perfect and trued. Making your fabric thread perfect means that the last crosswise thread at each end of your woven fabric can be pulled all the way across the width without breaking. There

are two methods for making your fabric thread perfect, and both are pretty easy.

The first method you can use is to tear quickly across the crosswise grain. Clip through the selvage about 1 in. Hold the fabric on each side of the clip firmly and pull to tear. Press the torn edge flat. Keep in mind that not all fabrics can be torn.

The second method is to pull a thread. This can be done on any woven fabric without distorting the grain or finish. Clip through the selvage about 1 in. From the clipped area, find a crosswise thread and pull it (it doesn't have to be removed, just dislodged enough to provide a

Most washable fabrics can be dry-cleaned. Dry-clean-only fabrics are not necessarily washable. Beware of warnings, special exceptions, and instructions. Be sure to pretreat your linings, interfacing, and any trims, too.

You can find the crossgrain of your fabric by clipping into the selvage, pulling a crosswise thread, and then cutting along it. When you pull, be sure to do so gently so that the thread doesn't break.

line to cut by), as shown in the photo above. Cut along the crosswise thread.

Now true the fabric by folding it in half lengthwise and matching the selvages. The two cut ends just straightened should form a right angle with the selvage. The fabric should be smooth and flat. Natural-fiber fabric can be steamed and gently tapped with the sole plate of the iron in a lengthwise and crosswise direction to achieve this.

Some fabrics acquire a permanent memory and resist alignment. These fabrics can be trued by making a lengthwise fold with selvages together and using an L-square to form a straight crosswise grain. Draw in the crossgrain on the wrong side using a fabric erasable marker or chalk, then cut on this line through both layers of fabric.

Fold knits as evenly as possible, making sure the ribs (comparable to lengthwise grain) are not twisted at the foldline. This fold will act as the straight-grain guide when pinning your pattern.

3 Getting the Right Fit

Your appearance is enhanced by how well your clothes fit. Most of us with less-than-ideal figures can direct attention away from figure variations if our clothes fit well. If you follow my fitting process, you will enjoy a sense of accomplishment and feel more self-confident in what you wear. Pants are not difficult to sew. However, fitting them on yourself can be frustrating. Even with a three-way mirror, you may see the problem, but reaching it and knowing how to correct it is another story.

Of all your garments, pants require the most intricate adjustment and fitting techniques. Commercial pattern adjustment lines do not always correspond to your body proportions. The pants can be too big or too small because ease amounts have been interpreted differently by you and by the designer. Your individual figure variances have not been addressed. The result is ill-fitting and uncomfortable pants.

In this chapter, personalizing your pattern and determining ease will be done by calculation instead of guesswork. Follow along as I lead you through the steps of measuring body and pattern so you can determine your fit before cutting your fabric. By working through this process you will be able to measure and adjust any pattern where fit is important.

Taking and Comparing Measurements

I am about 5 ft. 7 in. Although my back waist length measurement matches the pattern for my size, I am proportionally shorter on top and longer below my waist. Consequently, the length and proportion of a pants pattern is never correct for me. I always need to adjust it in several places. Pattern companies understand we all have curves in relatively standardized places, but the distance between these parts varies from one person to another.

I have taken the same basic style of pants with the same ease, detailing, and amount of darting from different pattern companies and made them up in the full range of sizes. In my fitting classes, it is interesting to see how the same size pattern from one pattern company fits different shapes. Also be aware that using the same size does not guarantee consistency of fit between companies. Having hand-drafted patterns as well as used computer-aided drafting programs, I'm not sure there is a "perfect" pattern. There are always some fitting refinements that can be done.

Pattern companies do not label patterns as thoroughly as I will have you label your pattern. By identifying specific body points and relating them to your pattern, you will have a better understanding of why specific adjustments are necessary and where to make them, regardless of the pattern you choose.

For those of you who've had pants fitting problems and those who have yet to sew your first pair of pants, when you understand why there are differences between your measurements and the pattern's, where they occur on the pattern and body, and how to correct them, you will be more likely to enjoy the measuring and adjusting process because you will then be successful in achieving a good fit. To start this process, you must first mark and measure your body. You will then repeat this on your pattern at the same points/positions as marked and measured on you.

Preparing to measure your body

Accurate measuring begins with a good foundation. For measuring, wear panty hose over any undergarments you will normally wear under your pants. Wear shoes that have the heel height you most often wear. When measuring, you will need to enlist the help of a friend and gather the following "tools":

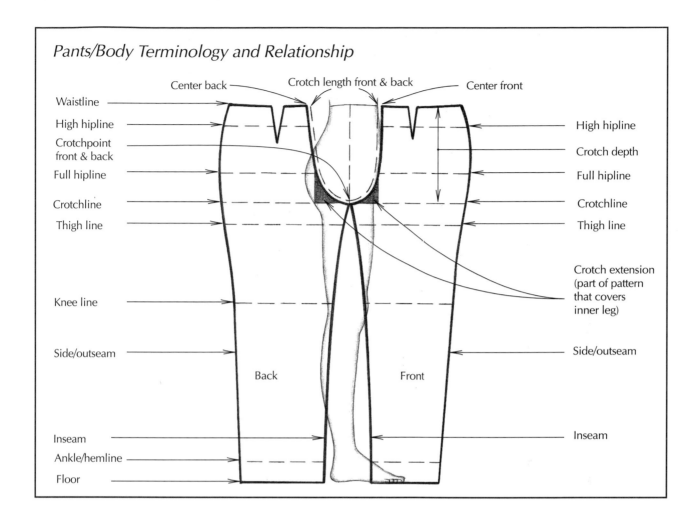

Pants/Body Terminology and Relationship

Center back

Crotch length front & back

Center front

Waistline

High hipline

Crotchpoint front & back

Full hipline

Crotchline

Thigh line

Knee line

Side/outseam

Back

Front

Inseam

Ankle/hemline

Floor

High hipline

Crotch depth

Full hipline

Crotchline

Thigh line

Crotch extension (part of pattern that covers inner leg)

Side/outseam

Inseam

- long mirror
- tape measure
- 4 pieces of ¼-in.-wide elastic that are long enough to fit around your hips
- ¾-in.- to 1 in.-wide Ban-Rol (not elastic) that is 4 in. longer than your waist measurement
- straight pins
- several pieces of ¼-in.-wide masking tape, each about 18 in. long
- Measurement Chart (see p. 38)

Establishing body reference points

You will now establish five key body reference points: waist, high hip, full hip, thigh, and knee. Later these same five reference points will be established on your pattern. You will then be able to compare your measurements with the pattern's measurements. Differences between your measurements and your pattern's will signal a need for a pattern adjustment. Measurements,

MEASUREMENT CHART

	MEASURE-MENTS	1 BODY	2 MINIMUM WEARING EASE	3 DESIGN EASE	4 I NEED (add columns 1, 2, and 3)	5 PATTERN	6 DIFFERENCE (+ you are larger; - you are smaller)	7 ADJUSTMENT AMOUNT (+ or -)
LENGTH	1. Crotch depth							
LENGTH	2. Waist to knee							
LENGTH	3. Waist to floor							
WIDTH	4. Waist		1½ in.					See chart on p. 52, col. 1 or 2
WIDTH	5. High hip ( )		1 in.					See chart on p. 52, col. 1 or 2
WIDTH	6. Full hip ( )		2 in.					See chart on p. 52, col. 1 or 2
WIDTH	7. Thigh ( )		2 in.					See chart on p. 52, col. 3
LENGTH	8. Crotch length							

observations, and analysis of your body will help you achieve the best fit (see the drawing on the facing page).

First, have your helper visually divide your side view in half using masking tape. Begin at the waist and go down to knee level (see the left photo on p. 40). This tape should divide your leg in half from waist to hem if the tape were extended that far.

Waist Establish your waist position by securing the Ban-Rol around your waist and snugging it to your personal degree of comfort. Pin it securely in place. Make sure the size is also comfortable while sitting. Readjust if necessary. Make sure you have positioned the Ban-Rol where you want your pants waistband to fit. The accuracy of all other measurements depends on the correct positioning of this reference point. Your waist is not

AN OVERVIEW OF MEASURING AND ADJUSTING PROCEDURES

This is an important and sequential process. Necessary pattern adjustments will be made based on a comparison of personal and pattern measurements. The accuracy and adjustments require that you follow this sequence.

1. Establish reference points on your body.

2. Measure your body. Record on your Measurement Chart.

3. Establish general reference points on the pattern.

4. Establish lengthening/shortening lines on the pattern.

5. Measure pattern lengths and compare them with your length measurements.

6. Make necessary length adjustments.

7. Establish your width levels (distance from waist) on pattern.

8. Measure pattern widths and compare with your width measurements.

9. Make necessary width adjustments.

10. Make refining adjustments that apply based on figure observations.

11. Measure the pattern crotch length.

12. Make crotch length adjustments.

13. True the pattern.

Body Measurements

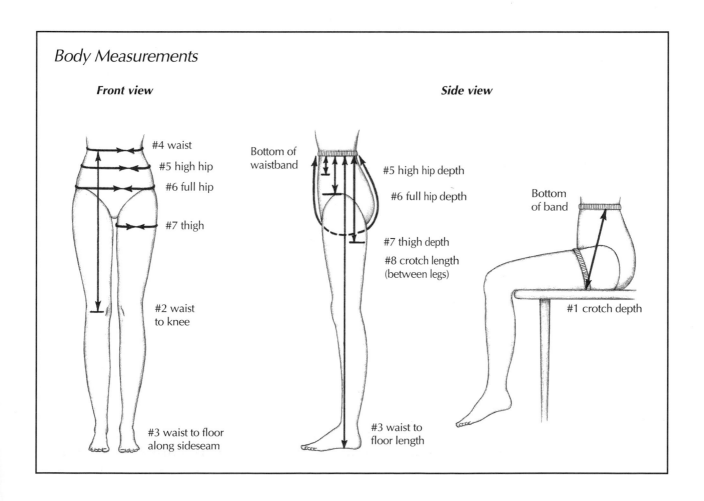

Front view

#4 waist
#5 high hip
#6 full hip
#7 thigh
#2 waist to knee
#3 waist to floor along sideseam

Side view

Bottom of waistband
#5 high hip depth
#6 full hip depth
#7 thigh depth
#8 crotch length (between legs)
#3 waist to floor length

Bottom of band
#1 crotch depth

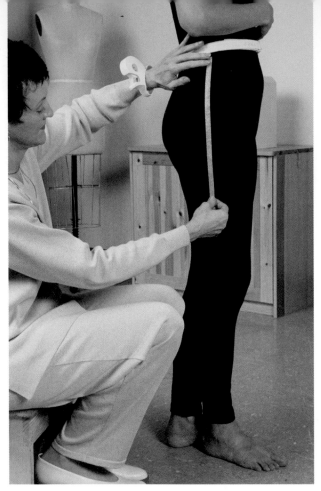

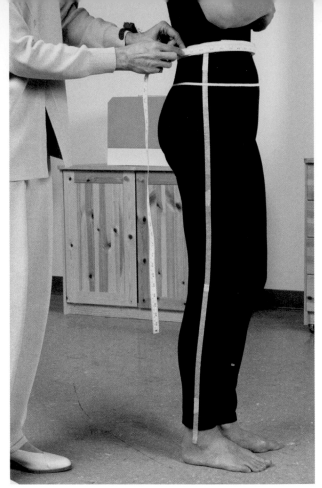

Before establishing your reference points, have a helper visually divide your side view in half with a piece of tape. This only needs to be done on one side.

The waist is measured over Ban-Rol. With elastic, mark the high-hip level parallel to the waist where the tummy protrudes the most at center front.

necessarily the top band of your panty hose or undergarment. Leave the band in place until all measurements have been completed. Always measure from the bottom of the Ban-Rol.

High hip If you do not have a tummy or are not fleshy in the area just below your waist, skip this step. If you are a bit fleshy here, turn sideways and determine the point on your abdomen where your tummy protrudes the most (the apex of the curve). Mark this point with a small piece of tape. Measure from the bottom of the Ban-Rol at center front to this point. Repeat this measuring and marking with tape the same distance at each side and at center back. Tie a piece of elastic around your waist at this level (see the right photo above). Pin the elastic to your undergarments at these four marks to prevent slippage.

Full hip Tie another piece of elastic around your body where

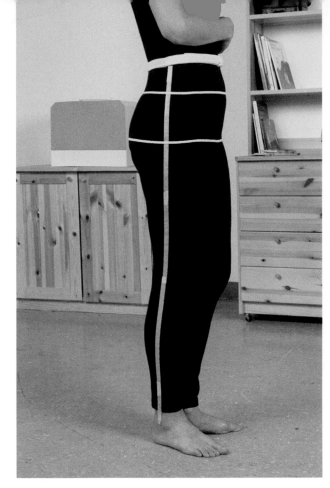

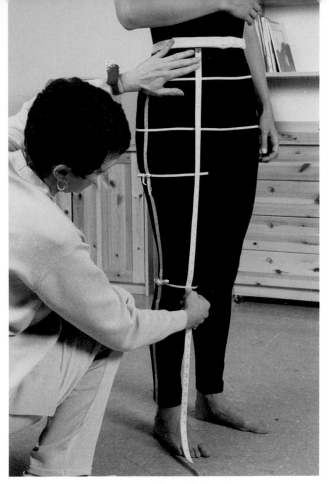

The full-hip line is parallel to the floor and at the level where the buttocks protrudes the most.

The middle of the knee is marked with elastic. The waist to knee measurement is taken down the center of the leg.

your buttocks protrudes the most. Position the elastic so it is parallel to the floor at the sides and back (see the left photo above). Pin the elastic to your undergarments at front, sides, and back.

Thigh Tie the third piece of elastic around one leg where your leg meets your torso.

Knee Tie the last piece of elastic around the leg at mid knee.

MEASURING FIVE REFERENCE POINTS

Use a purchased pair of pants as a guide for fit. Measure them just as you did for your body, in the same places. The more precise you are, the more accurate this fitting tool will be.

To figure crotch depth (measurement #1), measure the side seam from the bottom of the waistband or the natural waistline to the finished hemline. Measure the inseam. Subtract the inseam measurement from the side length. Note measurements for any other areas for which you like the fit. You may use different pants for different measurements. Also note the style of pants for each—jeans, slacks, or trousers.

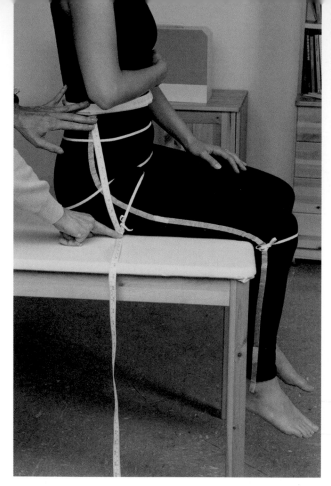

When measuring crotch depth, sit on a table with your knees against the edge. Measure from the side waist to the point where the thigh elastic meets the table.

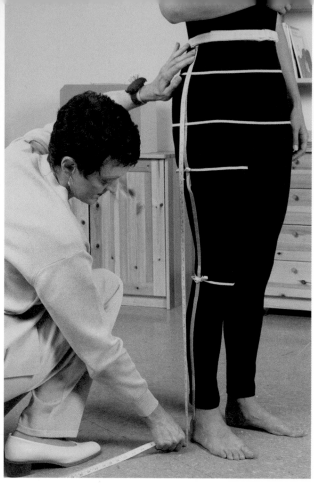

The waist-to-floor measurement is taken by following the body contour to hip level then dropping straight to the floor. Measure the right and left sides. Record the longer measurement.

Measuring length and width/circumference

Length and width measurements are arranged in the order adjustments will be made on your pattern, proceeding from the top to the bottom of the Measurement Chart (see p. 38).

After completing your measurements, you will make all pattern length adjustments except crotch length, beginning first with the crotch depth. An adjustment in the crotch depth will affect all other subsequent pattern length measurements. It is easier and more efficient if you proceed with your adjustments sequentially (follow numbers 1 through 7 in the left-hand column on the Measurement Chart on p. 38). After completing your pattern length adjustments, it's time for the width measurements. They are positioned at the same level (distance from waist) as measured on your body. The final measurement, crotch length, won't be made until after all of the other measurements are made.

Crotch depth You will need a table or countertop to sit on for this measurement. Adjust the thigh elastic so it is against your crotch at the inseam. The elastic should be parallel to the floor at the outside leg, so pin here if necessary to prevent movement. Sit up straight on a flat surface so that the backs of your knees are against the vertical edge. Measure on an angle from the side middle-waist marking to where the sitting surface and the elastic meet (see the right photo on p. 41). Record the measurement in column 1 of your Measurement Chart (see p. 38).

Waist to knee Measure down the middle front leg to the knee mark (see the left photo on the facing page). Record the measurement in column 1.

Waist to floor Measure the side length to the floor following the curve of your body to about hip level, then straight to the floor (see the right photo on the facing page). Measure both sides. Record the longer measurement in column 1.

Waist Measure the circumference of your waist over the Ban-Rol. Record the measurement in column 1. It is important to note here that although you may have a measurement of 30 in., that does not mean that 15 in. are proportioned from side to side in the front and 15 in. side to side in the back. You may be proportioned unevenly with, for example, 18 in. in the front and 12 in. in the back. If that's the case, then later, when making a waist adjustment on your pattern, add more width to the front, where it is needed, than the back. This will give a better balance to the side seam. If the adjustment amount is added equally to the front and back, the side seam will pull toward the front about waist level because the front part of the body needs more fabric.

High hip If you marked your high hip with a piece of elastic, walk the tape around the body at that level, holding it as you go to prevent it from slipping off the elastic line. Record the circumference in column 1. You should also make a notation of the distance from the waist, in the parentheses in the column titled Measurements (see the Measurement Chart on p. 38).

Full hip Repeat the same procedure as for high hip.

Thigh Adjust the leg elastic in the thigh area so it is parallel to the floor and around the fullest part. The positioning may be the same or different than when positioned for the crotch-depth measurement. Measure the thigh circumference at the elastic

PATTERN EASE CHART INTERPRETATION

PATTERN FIT DESCRIPTION	HIP FITTING EASE INCORPORATED	DESIGN EASE INCORPORATED	TOTAL PATTERN EASE INCLUDED
Close fitting	2 in.	0 in.	2 in.
Fitted	2 in.	1 in.	3 in.
Semi-fitted	2 in.	1 in. to 2 in.	3 in. to 4 in.
Loose fitting	2 in.	2 in. to 4 in.	4 in. to 6 in.
Very loose fitting	2 in.	Over 4 in.	Over 6 in.

level. Record the measurement in column 1. Measure from the bottom of the Ban-Rol along the side of the tape marking to the thigh elastic level. Make a notation of the distance from the waist in parentheses in the column titled Measurements (see the Measurement Chart on p. 38).

Crotch length Measure from the bottom of the Ban-Rol at center front to center back, between your legs. The tape should be lightly touching your body. Record the measurement in column 1.

Finishing up the Measurement Chart

Having finished all body length and width measurements, you are ready to complete column 4 on your Measurement Chart. All pants patterns designed for woven fabrics incorporate a minimum amount of wearing ease in the hip for movement and comfort. In addition to wearing ease, design ease is added to vary the style or look. Design ease includes extra fullness represented by gathers, pleats, tucks, or flare. For the full hip, refer to the chart above for the amount to enter in column 3—Design ease—of your Measurement Chart. To determine the approximate design ease that has been incorporated into your pattern, read the description on the back of your pattern envelope to give you a fitting clue. Choose the "inch" amount of design ease on the chart that corresponds to the pattern fit description. If there are no clues, carefully look at the style of your pants. Traditional jeans are usually close fitting; slacks are fitted or semi-fitted; trousers are loose; and styles that are very full or have wide legs are very loose fitting.

Put the tape measure around your full hip. To the tape measurement add 2 in. (minimum wearing ease). Then add the design ease amount for your particular pattern as determined on the chart. Is this the total amount of ease (fullness) you want in the hip area? Increase or decrease the amount of design ease to fit your personal preference. Record the amount of design ease you prefer or that corresponds to your pattern's fit description. Keep in mind this is additional ease in excess of the 2 in. you need for wearing comfort. If you change the design ease amount, you may be changing the style of the pants pattern as it was originally intended, in which case you should reevaluate your pattern choice. Trying to change your pattern into something it wasn't originally designed for can create more problems than you want to solve. Once you've determined

the ease measurements, add columns 1, 2, and 3 on your Measurement Chart, and record the totals in column 4.

Take a few minutes to make some observations about your figure. Look at your body from the front or back and side. Check those observations that correspond to your body (see the drawing on p. 46). These observed variances refer to the refining adjustments you need to make to your pattern after all length and width adjustments have been completed. Instructions for refining adjustments are included later in this chapter (see p. 58).

Establishing Pattern Reference Points

When you have completed marking and measuring your body, you are ready to do these same things on your pattern. Press your tissue pattern pieces with a warm, dry iron. Patterns are generally made and marked in one of the following ways: those that have seam allowances included and the seamline marked; those that do not have seam allowances included and therefore the seamline is not marked; and those that have seam allowances included but the seamline is not marked, as in multisized patterns. Look at your pattern to see if the seamline is

Figure Variations (Observations)

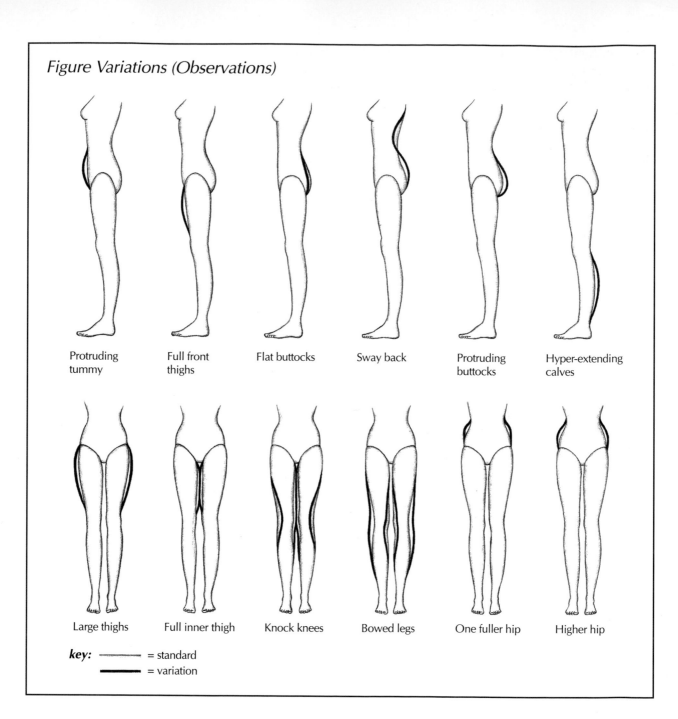

Protruding tummy

Full front thighs

Flat buttocks

Sway back

Protruding buttocks

Hyper-extending calves

Large thighs

Full inner thigh

Knock knees

Bowed legs

One fuller hip

Higher hip

key: ———— = standard

———— = variation

marked. A broken line inside the pattern cutting line will indicate this.

Preparing your pattern

If your pattern does not have the seamline marked but does include a seam allowance (usually ⅝ in.), make sure you confirm the amount of the seam allowance by looking on the pattern or in the instructional guide sheet included with your pattern. With multisized patterns, specific pattern pieces are marked with three or more distinctly different cutting lines for each size. Multisizing makes adjusting your pattern somewhat easier because you can transition from one line (size) to another while cutting. For example, if your waist is a size 12 but your hips are a 16, you would gradually cut toward the size 16 cutting line from the waist. Not all patterns come multisized. Therefore, I will guide you through marking similar reference points on your tissue pattern and measuring lengths and widths to determine what adjustments need to be made to correspond to your measurements. This will result in a more precise fit. Learning to do this will enable you to adjust any pattern, multisized or not.

If you have determined that your tissue pattern does not have the seamlines marked but does have seam allowances included, you will need to mark them by hand.

This may seem time-consuming, but it means that measuring your pattern later will be less confusing and easier. If your pattern doesn't include seam allowances or if the seamlines are marked, you can skip marking them in.

Seamlines should be marked along the following pattern edges: waist, side, inseam, and center front and center back through the crotch curve. If your seam allowance is ⅝ in. and your tape measure is ⅝ in. wide, lay it flat against the cutting line of your pattern to quickly mark the seamlines. If using a multisize pattern, use the same size line throughout the marking process. It is helpful to mark the seamlines in red. Dot or dash a line in. If your pattern includes a hem allowance (the amount is printed at the bottom of the pattern), measure up the allowance amount from the bottom edge of the pattern. Draw a line parallel to the bottom. This is the hemline. Extend the grainline arrows on the front and back tissue pattern the full length of the pattern.

To preserve your original pattern, make a copy of it before you start marking your reference points and adjustments on it.

Marking length reference lines

Not all patterns are identically and consistently marked. Therefore you may find that some of the following lines are already indicated on your pattern and some are not. Draw in the ones you don't have, as instructed, on the front and back pattern pieces.

Establish two pattern reference lines—the crotchline and the knee line. For the crotchline, draw a line from the crotch point to the side of the pattern, perpendicular to the pattern straight grain arrow (grainline). Label it crotchline. The knee line will be halfway between the crotchline and the hemline (if your pattern does not have a hem allowance included, the bottom of your pattern will be the hemline). Draw a line from the inseam to the side, perpendicular to the grainline. Label it knee line. These two lines will be used to determine pattern length measurements #1 and #2.

For pattern length adjustments you need three lines: one above the crotchline, one halfway between the crotchline and the knee line, and one halfway between the knee line and the hemline. The adjustment line above the crotch should be 2½ in. above the crotchline. Establish these adjustment (lengthening/shortening) lines if they are not included on your pattern. They should be perpendicular to the grainline and extend the width of each pattern piece. Label the above-

the-crotchline lengthening/shortening. Draw in and label the other two adjustment lines.

Measuring pattern lengths and making adjustments

Pattern length measurements and adjustments must be made now and done one at a time in the order listed on the Measurement Chart so that the pattern width measurements and adjustments will be made at the same level (distance from waist) each was measured on your body.

Record all pattern measurements in column 5 on your Measurement Chart. The procedure will be: measure the pattern, record the measurement, figure the difference between columns 4 and 5, record the difference in column 6. In column 7, record your pattern adjustment amount.

Crotch depth To measure crotch depth on the pattern, stand the tape measure on edge. Begin at the waist and follow the side curve of the pattern to the crotchline (see the drawing on the facing page). Once you have this measurement you can figure out the adjustment you'll need to make. Let's use the following example: Your body measurement (column 1) = 10¾ in. and the pattern crotch depth (column 5) = 11½ in. That means the adjustment is -¾ in. to shorten the pattern.

Establishing Pattern Reference Points for Length and Width

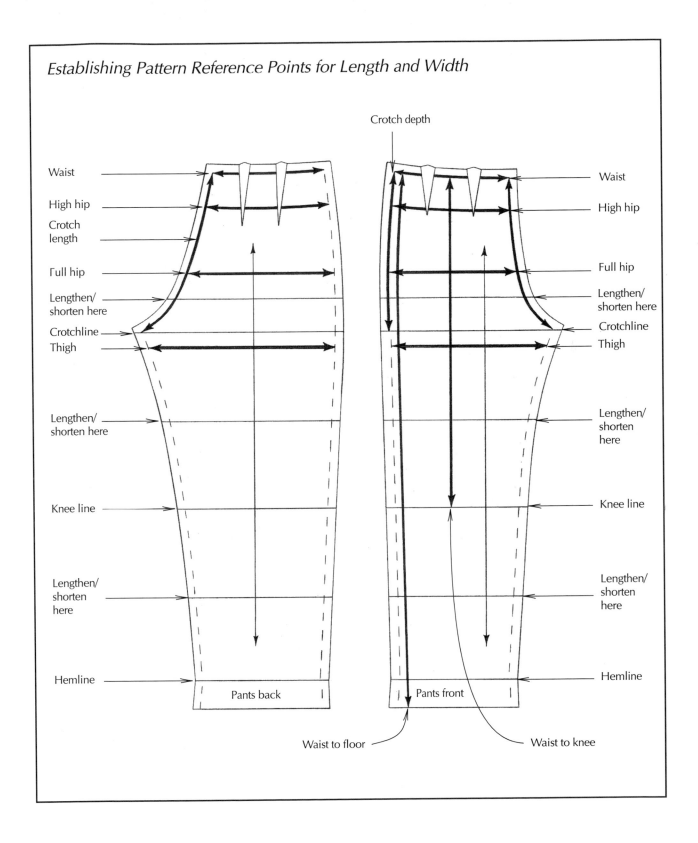

Waist

High hip

Crotch length

Full hip

Lengthen/ shorten here

Crotchline

Thigh

Lengthen/ shorten here

Knee line

Lengthen/ shorten here

Hemline

Pants back

Crotch depth

Waist

High hip

Full hip

Lengthen/ shorten here

Crotchline

Thigh

Lengthen/ shorten here

Knee line

Lengthen/ shorten here

Hemline

Pants front

Waist to floor

Waist to knee

Shortening (-) Crotch Depth

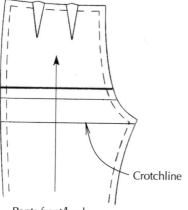

Pants front/back

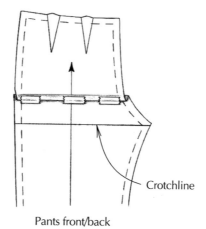

— Crotchline

Pants front/back

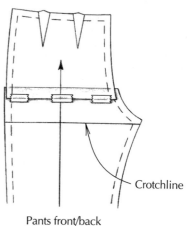

— Crotchline

Pants front/back

On the lengthening/shortening line above the crotchline, measure up the amount of adjustment on pattern front and back. Draw a line parallel to the lengthening/shortening line. Adjust by folding or by cutting.

• Crease on the newly drawn line and fold it down to meet the lengthening/shortening line. Tape in place.
OR

• Cut on the newly drawn line and match it to the lengthening/shortening line. Match grainlines and tape in place.

Lengthening (+) Crotch Depth

• Cut pattern apart on the lengthening/shortening line above the crotchline.
• Place paper under one pattern piece and tape in place.
• Measure from the cut edge of the pattern the amount of the adjustment. Draw a line on the added paper parallel to the cut edge of the taped pattern.
• Extend the grainline onto paper. Match the grainline and cut edge of untaped pattern piece to these lines and tape in place.

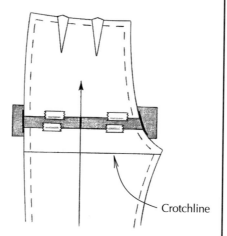

— Crotchline

Pants front/back

To shorten the crotch depth, measure up from the lengthening/shortening line above the crotchline the amount of the adjustment (see the drawing above). Draw a line parallel to the lengthening/shortening line. Adjust it in one of the following two ways:

• Crease on the newly drawn line and fold it down to meet the lengthening/shortening line. Tape in place.
• Cut on the newly drawn line and match it to the lengthening/shortening line, aligning the grainlines. Tape in place.

To lengthen the crotch depth, follow these steps (see the bottom drawing on the facing page):

1. Cut the pattern apart on the lengthening/shortening line above the crotchline. Tape a piece of see-through paper slightly wider than your pattern and longer than your adjustment to one edge of the cut-apart pattern.

2. Using added paper, measure from the cut edge of the pattern piece the adjustment amount, and draw a horizontal line parallel to the cut edge.

3. Extend the grainline onto the added paper.

4. Match up the grainline on the pattern to the extended grainline on the added paper, aligning the cut edge of the pattern you are joining with the horizontal adjustment line you added (see the photo above). Tape in place.

Waist to knee Measure from the waist to the knee line down the center of the front pants pattern (see the drawing on p. 49). Follow the same procedure to shorten or lengthen the pattern as for the crotch depth. The adjustment here is done on the lengthening/shortening line above the knee.

Waist to floor Stand the tape measure on edge and follow the side of the pattern from the waist to the bottom of the pattern (see the drawing on p. 49). Note: This measurement includes up to a 2-in. hem, which was allowed for in the body measurement. The finished length will be at the base of your ankle bone. If you want your pants longer, add the increased length amount to the adjustment amount in column 7. The adjustment will be done on the lengthening/ shortening line below the knee line. Refer to the crotch depth for adjustment instructions.

Measuring pattern widths and making adjustments

To accurately measure and adjust pattern widths to correspond to your body measurements, the adjustments must be positioned the same distance from the waist as measured on your body. Along the side, measure and mark the distance from the waist on the

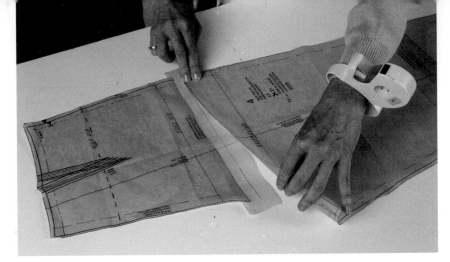

When making length adjustments, extending the grainline on the added paper makes realigning the pattern pieces more accurate while keeping the cut edges parallel.

PATTERN ADJUSTMENT AMOUNTS

Accuracy is in relation to purpose and provided as a convenience.

Difference (Measurement Chart column 6)	Column 1 Side adjustments for 2 in. or less	Column 2 Side, center front, and center back adjustments for more than 2 in.	Column 3 For thighs only: side and inside leg seam
INCHES	DIVIDED BY FOUR	DIVIDED BY EIGHT	DIVIDED BY FOUR
1	1/4	1/8	1/4
1 1/4	3/8	1/8	3/8
1 1/2	3/8	1/4	3/8
1 3/4	1/2	1/4	1/2
2	1/2	1/4	1/2
2 1/4		1/4	5/8
2 1/2		3/8	5/8
2 3/4		3/8	3/4
3		3/8	3/4
3 1/4		3/8	7/8
3 1/2		1/2	7/8
3 3/4		1/2	1
4		1/2	1
4 1/4		1/2	1 1/8
4 1/2		5/8	1 1/8
4 3/4		5/8	1 1/4
5		5/8	1 1/4
5 1/4		5/8	1 3/8
5 1/2		3/4	1 3/8
5 3/4		3/4	1 1/2
6		3/4	1 1/2
6 1/4		3/4	1 5/8
6 1/2		7/8	1 5/8
6 3/4		7/8	1 3/4
7		7/8	1 3/4
7 1/4		7/8	1 7/8
7 1/2		1	1 7/8
7 3/4		1	2
8		1	2
8 1/4		1	2 1/8
8 1/2		1 1/8	2 1/8
8 3/4		1 1/8	2 1/4
9		1 1/8	2 1/4
9 1/4		1 1/8	2 3/8
9 1/2		1 1/4	2 3/8
9 3/4		1 1/4	2 1/2
10		1 1/4	2 1/2

pattern front and back for high hip (if measured), full hip, and thigh. Draw a line across each pattern piece at the full hip and thigh that is perpendicular to the grainline and label each line. The high hip cannot be drawn in at this time and will be discussed later.

You are now going to measure the pattern width for the waist, high hip (if measured on your body), full hip, and thigh. These measurements will tell you the size your finished pants will be in these areas before you cut your fabric. Record all pattern measurements in column 5. The procedure is: measure the pattern, record the measurement in column 5, figure the difference between columns 4 and 5, record the difference in column 6, then refer to the chart on the facing page for column 7 adjustment amount.

Since the darts and/or pleats would normally be sewn, they must be folded and pinned closed on the pattern prior to measuring. If your pattern has pleats, check the pattern envelope picture to see how quickly they dissipate down the front into little or no fullness. The fullness should be pinned closed at the waist by matching the pleat lines. Continue pinning the pleat closed down the leg, gradually dissipating the amount taken up by the pleat to zero (usually about crotchline level). Determine this level from

Before measuring for width, pin darts and pleats closed. Measure between the seam allowances with the tape measure on edge to get an accurate reading.

your pattern envelope or personal preference. With the darts and/or pleats pinned, draw in the line for the high hip from side edge to center front and center back, keeping distance parallel to waist.

To determine the finished width measurements of your pattern, begin by measuring the waist. Sometimes the finished-garment waist and full-hip size are printed on the front pattern piece, but not always. If not, stand the tape measure on edge and follow the curve of the waist (see the photo above). Add the front and back measurements and multiply by two. Repeat these measuring and recording instructions for the high hip, if measured on your body, and full hip. Total increases or decreases of 2 in. or less will be done equally at the sides on front and back. Increases or decreases of more than 2 in. will be done equally at the sides, center front, and center back.

To make width adjustments easy, use precut widths of adding machine or fax paper when adding extra paper to increase your pattern, or tape your front and back pattern pieces to a large sheet of tissue or sketch paper. In either case, the paper should be several inches larger than your greatest increase to allow for the truing (redrawing) of all pattern lines interrupted in the adjusting process.

Unpin all pleats and darts so your pattern is flat.

The final pattern width measurement will be for the thigh. Measure on the thigh line across the pattern front and back. Add the two measurements and record the total in column 5. Thigh adjustments will be made equally at the side seam and inseam on the front and back of the pattern.

Waist increase/decrease If your waist adjustment is a total of 2 in. or less (½ in. or less to each side seam), adjust each side at

waist level (see the left drawing below). Measure out from the pattern edge for an increase or measure in for a decrease. If your adjustment is a total of more than 2 in., adjust at each side, center front, and center back (see the right drawing below).

Waistband adjustments For a side-closing waistband with a total increase/decrease of 2 in. or less, add or subtract half the total amount of the increase or decrease at the side-seam marking in the middle of the waistband piece. On the ends, add or subtract one-quarter the

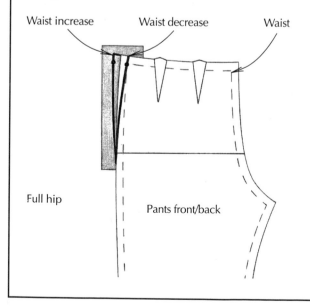

Waist Increase/Decrease of 2 in. or Less

Make the adjustment at each side on the front and back at the same level as the waist seam. Measure out from the cutting line for an increase or in onto the pattern for a decrease. The newly drawn line will become your cutting line.

Waist increase   Waist decrease   Waist

Full hip   Pants front/back

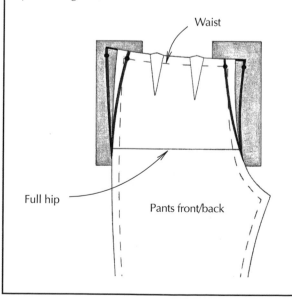

Waist Increase/Decrease of More Than 2 in.

If total increase/decrease is more than 2 in., divide the total increase/decrease by 8. Make the increase/decrease at side, center front, and center back. Use chart on p. 52 with Measurement Chart. Newly drawn lines become your cutting lines.

Waist

Full hip   Pants front/back

total amount at each side-seam marking (see the drawing below).

For a side-closing waistband with a total increase/decrease of more than 2 in., add or subtract one-quarter the total amount of the increase or decrease at the side-seam marking, center front, and center back. On the ends, add one-eighth the total amount at each side-seam marking.

For a center-front-closing/center-back-closing waistband with a 2-in. or less total increase/decrease, add or subtract half the total amount of the increase or decrease at each side-seam marking.

Waistband Adjustments

Side-closing waistband

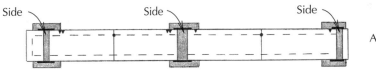

A. For a side-closing waistband with 2-in. or less increase/decrease: Add or subtract one-half the total amount of the increase/decrease to one side seam. On ends (left), add or subtract one-quarter the total amount to each side seam marking.

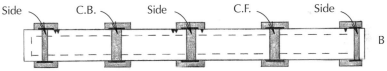

B. For a side-closing waistband with more than 2-in. increase/decrease: Add or subtract one-quarter the total amount of the increase/decrease to one side seam, center front, and center back. On the side with the closure (left), add one-eighth the total amount to each side-seam marking.

Center-back/ center-front-closing waistband

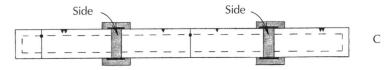

C. For a C.B./C.F.-closing waistband with 2-in. or less increase/decrease: Add or subtract one-half the total amount of the increase/decrease to each side seam.

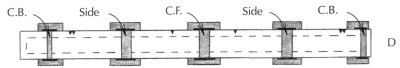

D. For a C.B.-closing waistband with more than 2-in. increase/decrease: Add or subtract one-quarter the total amount of the increase/decrease to center front and both side seams. At center back on each end add one-eighth the total amount of increase/decrease. Reverse this process for a C.F. closure.

High-Hip Increase/Decrease of 2 in. or Less

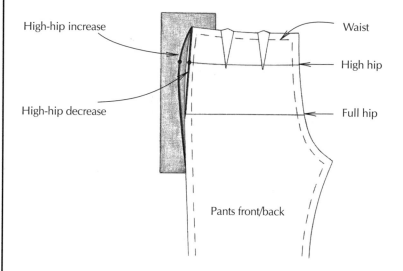

High-hip increase

High-hip decrease

Waist

High hip

Full hip

Pants front/back

To accommodate a more prominently curved figure just below the waist, add your high-hip adjustment amount from column 7 of your Measurement Chart to the side of the pattern. Add the increase at your personal high-hip distance from waist (amount in parentheses). A newly curved line between the waist and the full hip should incorporate this increase. To decrease, simply straighten the curve between the waist and full hip.

High-Hip Increase/Decrease of 2 in. or More

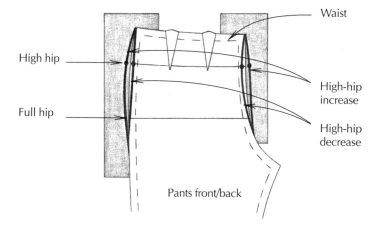

Waist

High hip

High-hip increase

Full hip

High-hip decrease

Pants front/back

This adjustment will be done the same way as for the 2-in. or less adjustment except in addition to the change made at the side, the adjustment amount from column 7 on your Measurement Chart will also be made at the center front and back. To decrease, simply straighten the curve between the waist and full hip at each side, center front, and center back.

For a center-back-closing waistband with more than a 2-in. total increase/decrease, add or subtract one-quarter the total amount of the increase or decrease to the center front and each side-seam marking. At the center back at each end, add one-eighth the total amount of the increase or decrease. Reverse the adjustment for a center-front-closing waistband.

High-hip increase/decrease If your high-hip adjustment is 2 in. or less, make an increase or decrease at high-hip level (see the top drawing at left). Usually this type of increase/decrease will accompany a waist increase/decrease, in which case the blending of your new side line from the waist adjustment will automatically adjust the high hip. Some women may be more fleshy below the waist or have a "roll," which will necessitate a high-hip adjustment. Refer to your Measurement Chart for the amount and placement (distance from waist) of this adjustment. If your adjustment is more than 2 in., adjust at each side, center front, and center back (see the bottom drawing at left).

A decrease in the high hip can cause an undesirable hollow along the side seam. To avoid creating this hollow, your adjustment should only involve straightening the curve at the high hip, not curving inward from the pattern edge.

Full-hip increase/decrease If your adjustment is a total of 2 in. or less, follow these steps (see the drawing at right):

1. At your marked full-hip level, measure out or in the adjustment amount from column 7 on your Measurement Chart.

2. Draw a curved line between the waist and full-hip adjustment. The more the increase, the greater the curve. Blend the line into the edge of the pattern smoothly. This may add a slight amount to the leg width, but it will look better proportionally. There is no increase/decrease in the leg width at the hemline.

If your adjustment total is more than 2 in., follow these steps (see the drawing on p. 58):

1. At your full-hip level, each side, center front, and center back, measure out or in from the edge of your pattern the adjustment amount from column 7 on your Measurement Chart.

2. Blend a line between the waist, full hip, and the original pattern edge at the hemline. There is no increase/decrease in the leg width at the hemline.

3. At the center front and center back, blend a line between the waist and crotch point.

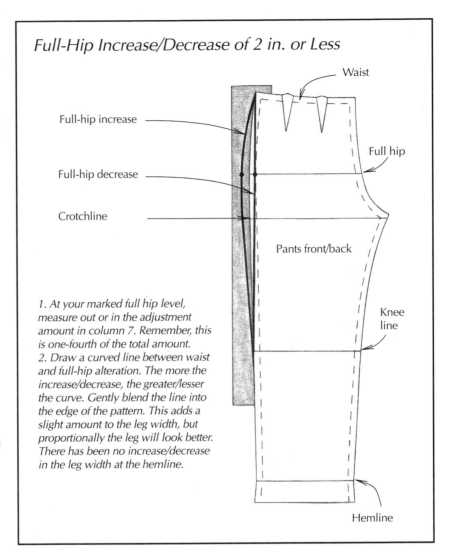

Full-Hip Increase/Decrease of 2 in. or Less

Waist

Full-hip increase

Full-hip decrease

Crotchline

Full hip

Pants front/back

Knee line

1. At your marked full hip level, measure out or in the adjustment amount in column 7. Remember, this is one-fourth of the total amount.
2. Draw a curved line between waist and full-hip alteration. The more the increase/decrease, the greater/lesser the curve. Gently blend the line into the edge of the pattern. This adds a slight amount to the leg width, but proportionally the leg will look better. There has been no increase/decrease in the leg width at the hemline.

Hemline

4. To balance the leg, draw a new inseam line, beginning at the crotch point. Add the same amount as you added to the side when blending. Taper to edge of pattern at the hemline.

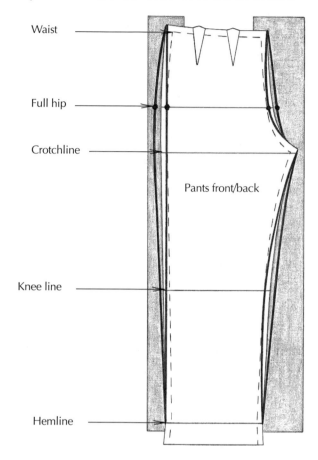

Full-Hip Increase/Decrease of 2 in. or More

Waist

Full hip

Crotchline

Pants front/back

Knee line

Hemline

1. At your full-hip distance from waist, measure out or in the adjustment amount from column 7 on your Measurement Chart at the side, center front, and center back.
2. Blend a line between the waist, full hip, and original pattern edge at the hemline. No width has been added or subtracted at the hemline.

3. At center front and center back, blend a line between the waist and crotch point.
4. To balance the leg, draw a line from the crotch point, adding the same amount at the knee that was added at the side and tapering to the hemline so there is no increase there.

Thigh increase/decrease Add or subtract the adjustment amount at your thigh distance from waist and at the side and inseam of the front and back. Add or subtract the same

amount at the crotch point that you added or subtracted at the inseam thigh level, tapering to nothing at the hemline (see the left drawing on the facing page).

Refining Adjustments

Refining adjustments are less common than pattern adjustments but not less important. They address the individual figure variations that you observed on your figure from the front and side (see the drawing on p. 46). These observations should have been checked after your measurements were completed.

Determining if an adjustment is necessary before cutting your fabric will depend on the closeness of fit for your style of pants, as well as the degree of variation. The closer the fit or the more particular you are about fit, the more important these adjustments become. The fit of other pants can give clues about where there are problem areas. Because there are no hard-and-fast rules, judgment is required. Therefore, refining the fit of your adjustments in a trial pair of pants is recommended to learn what amounts are best for you.

Here are some hints for making refining adjustments:
• Always place extra paper, preferably see-through, under cut portions of the pattern.

Thigh Increase/Decrease

Increase or decrease the adjustment amount at your thigh, at the side, and at the inseam of the front and back. You will add or subtract at the crotch point the same amount that you added/subtracted at the inseam thigh level, and taper to "0" at the hemline.

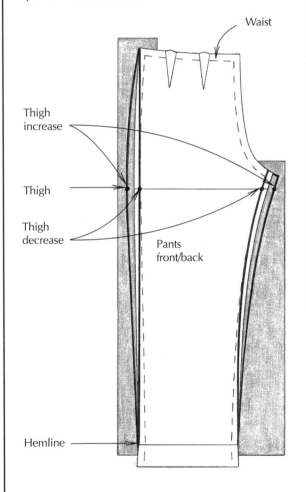

Waist

Thigh
increase

Thigh

Thigh
decrease

Pants
front/back

Hemline

Full Front Thigh

Add adjustment increase at your thigh distance from waist at the front seam crotch point and inseam only. Blend a new line along the side seam, adding "0" at the waist and hemline. Blend a new line from the crotch point and thigh line, tapering to "0" at the hemline.

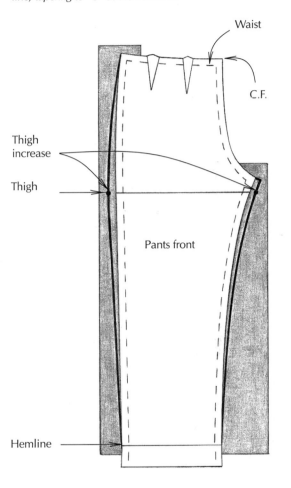

Waist

C.F.

Thigh
increase

Thigh

Pants front

Hemline

- Work on a flat surface that you can pin into, such as a foam, blocking, or ironing board.
- Adjust the pattern by moving or spreading it the needed amount.

- Control pattern movement by pinning the pattern to the working surface/board.
- Tape the pattern in place only after you are satisfied with the adjustment amount and the pattern is flat.

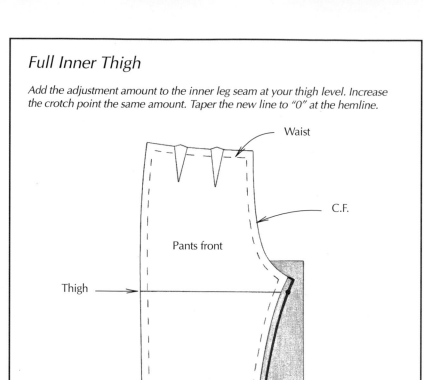

Full Inner Thigh

Add the adjustment amount to the inner leg seam at your thigh level. Increase the crotch point the same amount. Taper the new line to "0" at the hemline.

Waist

C.F.

Pants front

Thigh

Hemline

Full front thigh

To accommodate a full front thigh, increase at the front side and inseam at thigh distance from waist (see the right drawing on p. 59). Increase the crotch

point the same amount the inseam is increased. Blend a new line along the side, adding nothing at the waistline and hemline. Blend a line from the crotch point and thigh line, tapering to nothing at the hemline.

Full inner thigh

For a full inner thigh, increase the inseam at thigh level (see the drawing at left). Increase the crotch point the same amount. Taper to nothing at the hemline.

Protruding tummy

To accommodate a protruding tummy, you'll need to make a few changes. If your pattern has a fly-front zipper extension, cut it off along the center-front line (you will reattach it later). Because the body is curved at the center front, more length and width will be needed. However, little or nothing may need to be added at the side since tummy fullness dissipates toward the side. To adjust for a full tummy, follow these steps (see the drawing on the facing page):

1. At the high hip, cut from center front past the dart. Continue to cut but angle up to the side waist. *Do not* separate the pattern pieces at the seam.

Protruding Tummy

A tummy needs slightly more length and width at center front.

1. Cut horizontally on the high-hip line from center front past the dart or pleat, then angle up to the side waist.

2. Cut through the center of the dart or pleat from the waist down to within 1/16 in. of the high-hip cutting line.

3. Move the upper portion of the pattern (high hip to waist) up so the spread at center front is about 1/2 in. Let darts spread open slightly so the cutting line on the upper and lower pattern remains somewhat parallel and the pattern is flat. Redraw the darts, restoring them to their original length.

4. Redraw center front, blending a line between the waist and crotch curve.

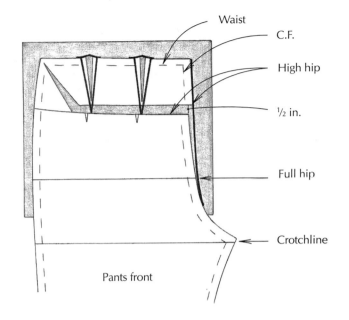

2. Cut through the center of the dart(s) to but not through the horizontal high-hip cut.

3. Spread the upper part of the pattern (the smaller part) at the center front 1/2 in.—slightly more for very large tummies, less for smaller ones. A little does a lot. This spreading will cause the center front above the high hip to jut out further, the darts to increase in size, and the front crotch length to become longer. Pin and tape the pattern in place. Redraw darts.

4. Redraw the center front. You can make this line an ever-so-gentle curve or keep it straight. If your pattern had a fly extension, make the same spread on it. Pin and tape in place. Then redraw your lines on the center-front fly extension to match the center front of the pants.

Protruding buttocks

Protruding, or full, buttocks can cause pants to pull and feel uncomfortable in the crotch. Side seams pull toward the back because more width is required

Protruding Buttocks

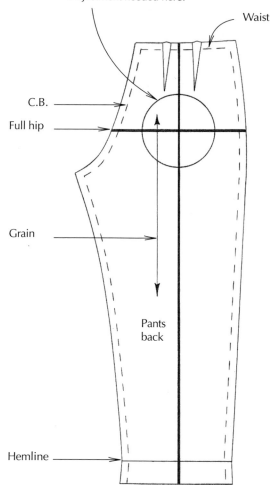

Adjustment needed here.

Waist

C.B.

Full hip

Grain

Pants back

Hemline

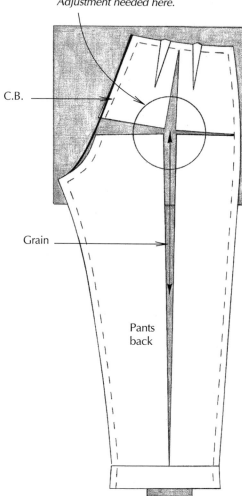

Adjustment needed here.

C.B.

Grain

Pants back

Full buttocks need more length at the center back and more width at the full hip.
On the pants back only:
1. Find the center of your horizontal full-hip line.
2. Draw a vertical line from the waist to hem that is parallel to the grainline and passes through the middle hip mark.
3. Cut the hipline from center back to side. Do not separate the pattern pieces at the side.
4. On the center vertical line, cut up to the waist and down to the hem. Do not separate the pattern pieces.
5. Spread $1/2$ in. to $1 1/2$ in. on the vertical line at mid hip.
6. Redraw the grainline if needed.
Blend the center back line between the waist and crotch curve.

across the back. To fix this problem, the crotch length needs to be increased, as does the width across the back. To make these adjustments on your back pattern, follow these steps (see the drawing on the facing page):

1. Find the center of the horizontal line at your full hip and mark.

2. Draw a line perpendicular to the full-hip line from the top to the bottom of your pattern, passing through the midpoint established in step 1.

3. On the full-hip line, cut from the center back to the side. *Do not* separate the pattern pieces at the side.

4. Beginning at the full-hip line, cut up and down the vertical line drawn in step 2. *Do not* separate the pattern pieces.

5. On the vertical line, spread the pattern at the full-hip level up to 1½ in. for a very full figure. Spread the lower portion of your pattern at the full-hip line first. Pin, then tape in place. Spread the upper portion the same amount at the full-hip level. The upper portion of the pattern moves up and away from the lower portion so there is a slight angular spread between the mid hip and side on the horizontal cutting line. Pin and tape in place.

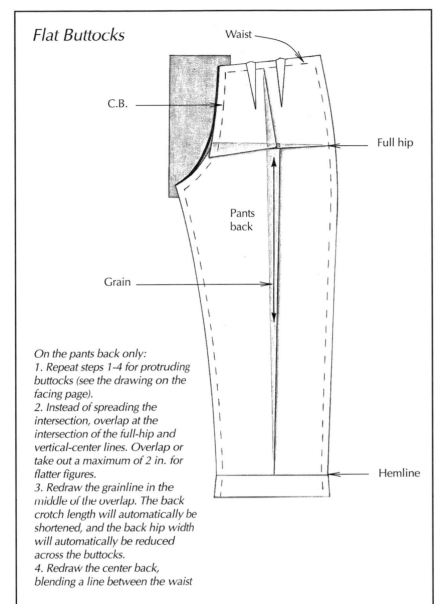

Flat Buttocks

Waist

C.B.

Full hip

Pants back

Grain

Hemline

On the pants back only:
1. Repeat steps 1-4 for protruding buttocks (see the drawing on the facing page).
2. Instead of spreading the intersection, overlap at the intersection of the full-hip and vertical-center lines. Overlap or take out a maximum of 2 in. for flatter figures.
3. Redraw the grainline in the middle of the overlap. The back crotch length will automatically be shortened, and the back hip width will automatically be reduced across the buttocks.
4. Redraw the center back, blending a line between the waist

6. Redraw the grainline in the middle of the spread if needed. The back crotch length and hip width has been increased. Redraw center back by blending a smooth line between the waist and midpoint of the crotch curve.

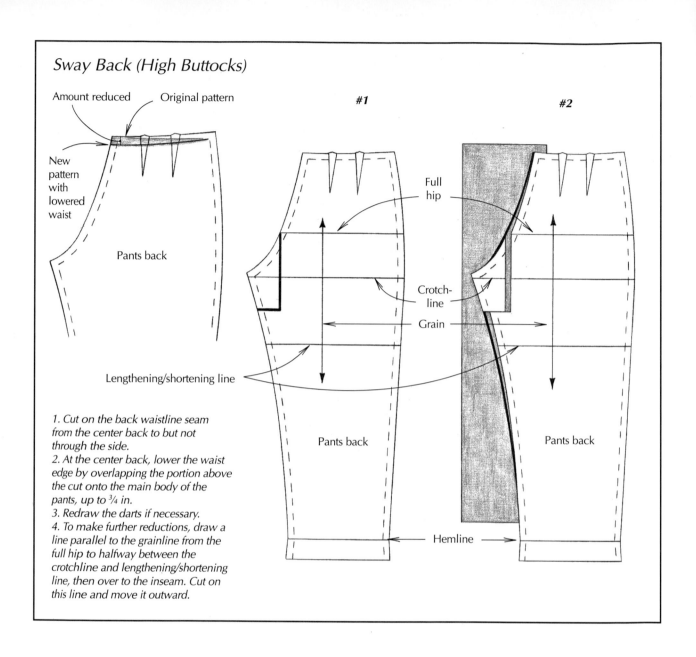

Sway Back (High Buttocks)

Amount reduced

Original pattern

New pattern with lowered waist

Pants back

Lengthening/shortening line

#1

Full hip

Crotch-line

Grain

Pants back

Hemline

#2

Pants back

1. Cut on the back waistline seam from the center back to but not through the side.
2. At the center back, lower the waist edge by overlapping the portion above the cut onto the main body of the pants, up to ¾ in.
3. Redraw the darts if necessary.
4. To make further reductions, draw a line parallel to the grainline from the full hip to halfway between the crotchline and lengthening/shortening line, then over to the inseam. Cut on this line and move it outward.

Flat buttocks

Flat buttocks need the opposite pattern adjustment of protruding buttocks. Less crotch length and width across the back is needed to avoid a back leg that is too full and droops under the buttocks. Follow the instructions for protruding buttocks but with

the following differences (see the drawing on p. 63):

1. After cutting on the full hip and drawing a vertical line (step 3 on p. 63), overlap up to 2 in. on the lower portion of your pattern at the full-hip level. Pin and tape in place. Repeat this same overlap on the upper portion of the pattern at the full-hip level. Pin and tape in place.

2. Redraw the grainline in the middle of the overlap. The back crotch length has automatically been shortened, and the back hip and leg taken in to reduce bagginess.

Sway back (high buttocks)

With a sway back, the distance between the full hip and waist is shorter at center back than at the sides, so a small fold of fabric just under the waistband but above the high hip will form at the center back. This fold will dissipate toward the side seam. To adjust your pattern to eliminate this problem (see the drawing on the facing page):

1. Cut on the waistline seam from the center back to but not through the side. If your pattern does not include seam allowances, measure down from center back waist a maximum of ¾ in. Fold dart(s) closed and blend a new line between center back mark and side waist intersection. With dart(s) closed, cut on newly drawn line.

2. Lower the waist edge by overlapping the portion above the cut onto the main body of the pants up to ¾ in. Pin and tape in place.

3. Redraw darts if necessary.

4. If more reduction is required, widen the back crotch area. To do this, draw a line parallel to the grainline from the center-back full-hip line to halfway between the crotchline and the lengthening/shortening line, then over to the inseam. Cut on this line and move the piece outward, parallel to the cut to compensate for the shortened crotch length. Pin and tape in place.

One fuller hip

A full hip, meaning one side of your body is slightly more fleshy than the other, can be accounted for in the fitting process of the fabric pants. Frequently a full hip can add length between the waist and full-hip lines. If diagonal wrinkles are visible between the crotch and high hip on pants in your current wardrobe, follow these steps to make a pattern adjustment (see the drawing on p. 66).

1. Make a copy of the front and back of your pattern from the crotchline up. Because you are changing only one side, you will have the original pattern for the unadjusted side and the adjusted pattern for the fuller hip. Label front and back copy right or left to correspond to the side being adjusted.

2. On the front and back copy draw a line parallel to the grainline between the side and the dart or pleat from the waist

One Fuller Hip

Frequently one hip tends to be slightly fuller than the other. The fullness can be removed in the fitting process if it is not excessive.

Because this is a change to only one side of the body, make a copy of your pattern from the crotchline up. This way you will have the original pattern for your straighter side and the adjusted one for the fuller side.

On the front and back of the side with the fuller hip:
1. Draw a vertical line parallel to the grainline between the side and the dart or pleat from the waist to the full hip, then on an angle to the intersection of the lengthening/shortening line and side.
2. From the side, cut in on the high-hip line, then up to the waist on the vertical line. Do not separate the pattern pieces at the waist.
3. Cut down to the full hip, then over to the side. Do not separate the pattern pieces at the side.
4. Spread the side at the seamline by the amount of the adjustment.

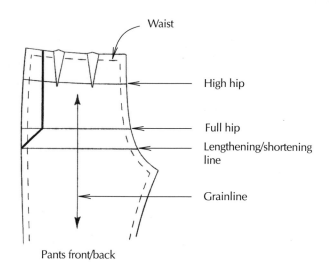

Pants front/back

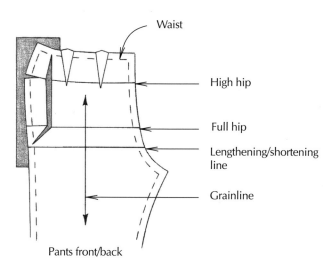

Pants front/back

edge of the pattern to the full-hip line, then on an angle to the intersection of the lengthening/shortening line and side.

3. From the side, cut in on the high-hip line, then up to the waist edge and down to the side on the drawn line. *Do not separate the pattern pieces at the side.*

4. Spread the side ¼ in. to ½ in. Pin and tape in place. If this is too much spread, it can be removed in the fitting process.

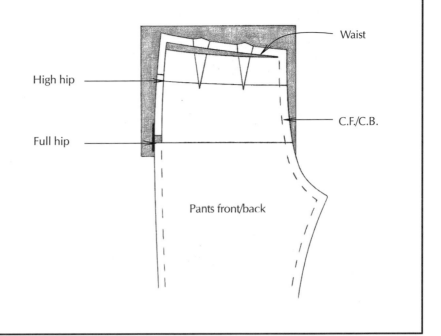

High Hip Only

1. On the front and back, cut in from the side on the full-hip line, and follow the seamline cut up to the waist seam and over to the center front and center back.

2. Raise the side seam at the waist seam the amount of the difference between right and left full-hip depth measurements.

Waist

High hip

Full hip

C.F./C.B.

Pants front/back

High hip only

If no wrinkling between high hip and crotch is evident on your current pants, but there is a difference between the waist-to-full-hip measurements of your right and left sides, make a copy of your pattern as in step 1 of the directions for one fuller hip. Continue with the following steps (see the drawing above):

1. On front and back at full-hip level, cut in ⅝ in., then up to the waist and over to center front and center back. The cut should be parallel to the pattern edge and ⅝ in. away from it.

2. Reestablish your waist level with Ban-Rol. Measure the left and right sides from your waist to the full hip. Use the amount of the difference between the two sides as a guide to spread your pattern in step 3.

3. Raise the side at the waist by the amount of the difference between the right and left waist-to-full-hip measurements as determined in step 2. Pin and tape in place. If your pattern does not include a seam allowance, raise the waist at the side equal to the amount of your adjustment and draw a new line between this point and the center front and back.

Knock knees

If the knees curve in slightly or touch, more width and length is required on the inseam. To make

Knock Knees

When the knees curve in slightly, more width and length is required at the inseam than at the side seam.
1. Cut on the lengthening/shortening line that's between the knee line and the crotchline. Move the lower portion of the pants leg toward the inseam. The amount will depend on figure deviation.
2. To increase the length on the inseam, cut on the lengthening/ shortening line that's below the knee line. Cut up the center of the bottom leg portion. Move half of the leg portion closest to the inseam down to increase the length. You may find ½ in. or less is necessary.
3. Redraw the hemline and lower edge of pattern, keeping the lines parallel.
4. Redraw the grainlines, extending the lower-leg grain toward the top.

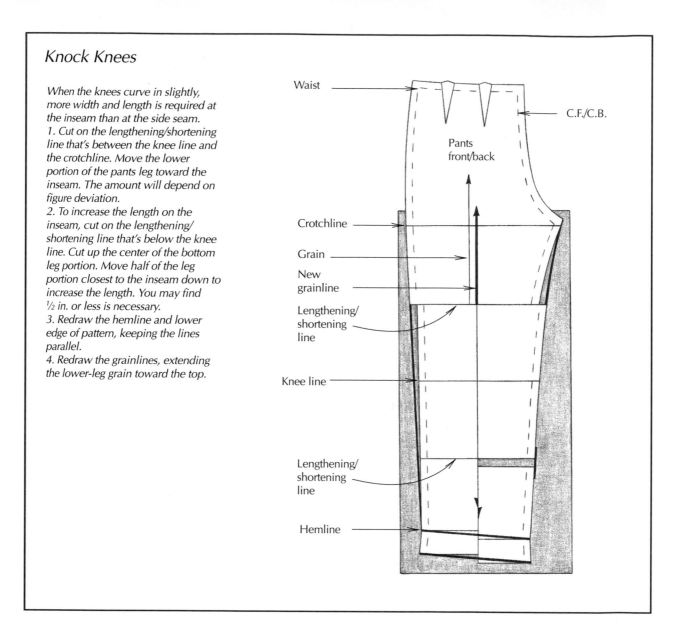

this easy adjustment see the drawing above:

1. Cut on the lengthening/ shortening line above the knee line but below the crotchline on front and back. Move the lower portion of the pants leg toward the inseam. Add about 1 in. for knees that are very curved (to the point of touching), and decrease the amount proportionately the slighter the curve. You may need to add more during the fitting stage. Pin and tape in place.

2. To increase the length on the inseam, cut on the lengthening/shortening line

Bowed Legs

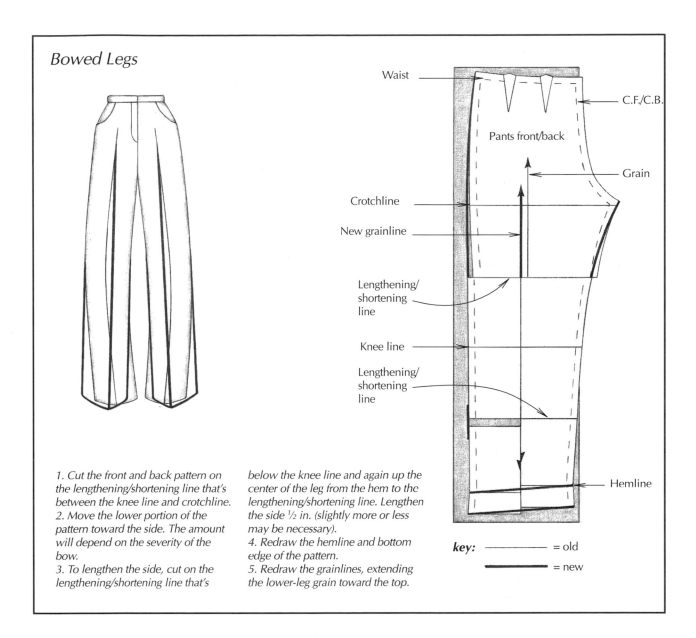

Waist

C.F./C.B.

Pants front/back

Grain

Crotchline

New grainline

Lengthening/
shortening
line

Knee line

Lengthening/
shortening
line

Hemline

key: ——————— = old
———— = new

1. Cut the front and back pattern on the lengthening/shortening line that's between the knee line and crotchline.
2. Move the lower portion of the pattern toward the side. The amount will depend on the severity of the bow.
3. To lengthen the side, cut on the lengthening/shortening line that's

below the knee line and again up the center of the leg from the hem to the lengthening/shortening line. Lengthen the side ½ in. (slightly more or less may be necessary).
4. Redraw the hemline and bottom edge of the pattern.
5. Redraw the grainlines, extending the lower-leg grain toward the top.

located below the knee line on front and back. Cut up the center of the bottom leg portion. Move the leg portion closest to the inseam down + or - ½ in. Pin and tape in place.

3. Redraw the hemline between side and inseam and the lower edge of the pattern. Lines should be parallel.

4. Redraw the grainline on front and back as one continuous line.

Hyperextended Calves

If you have hyperextended calves, you may notice a wrinkling or sagging of fabric just above the back knee. This can also be caused by posture. To correct this problem, try making these changes.

1. On the back only, measure up from the lengthening/ shortening line that's between the knee line and crotchline a maximum of ½ in. Draw a parallel line.

2. Crease on the lengthening/ shortening line and bring it up to meet the newly drawn line, or cut on the lengthening/ shortening line and bring the lower portion of the pattern up to meet the new line. Pin and tape in place.

3. Draw a line halfway between the lengthening/ shortening line and between the knee line and the hemline.

4. Cut on the line drawn in step 3 above, and lengthen the pattern the amount you shortened in steps 1 or 2 above.

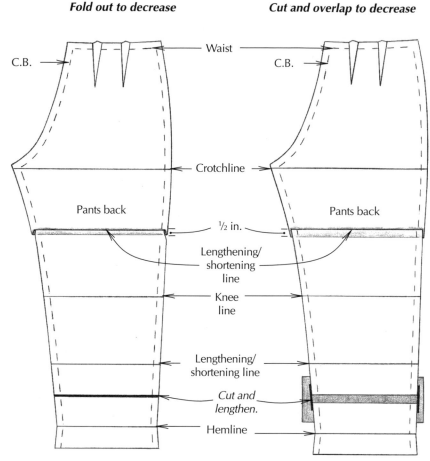

Fold out to decrease   **Cut and overlap to decrease**

C.B. — Waist — C.B.

— Crotchline —

Pants back   Pants back

½ in.

Lengthening/ shortening line

Knee line

Lengthening/ shortening line

Cut and lengthen.

Hemline

Bowed legs

Legs that curve outward above and below the knee require more width and length along the side. It is the opposite problem of knock knees (see the drawing on p. 69).

1. Cut the front and back pattern on the lengthening/ shortening line located between the knee and crotchline.

2. Move the lower portion of the pattern toward the side about 1 in. for a severe bow and less for minor curvature. Pin and tape in place.

3. Lengthen the side by cutting from the side on the lengthening/shortening line below the knee and down the center of the leg to the bottom of the pattern. Spread the side + or - ½ in., depending on the severity of the bow. Pin and tape in place.

4. Redraw the hemline between the side and inseam. Redraw the bottom of the pattern parallel to the hemline.

5. Redraw the grainline so it is one continuous line.

Hyperextended calves

Before doing this adjustment, recheck your side view and make sure you were not standing with your knees locked when the measurements and observations were made. If you have well-developed calf muscles, or if you consistently lock you knees when you stand, you may want to proceed with this adjustment. Here are the steps (see the drawing on the facing page):

1. On the back only, measure up from the lengthening/shortening line located between the knee and the crotchline a maximum of ½ in. Draw a parallel line.

2. Crease or cut on the lengthening/shortening line and bring it up to meet the newly drawn line to remove the excess. Pin and tape in place.

3. Draw a line halfway between the hemline and the lengthening/shortening line just above it.

4. Cut on this line, and lengthen the pattern by the amount you shortened above the knee. Pin and tape in place.

Crotch Length Adjustments

The final pattern measurement and adjustment will be for crotch length (see the drawing on p. 72). If you measured your pattern before completing adjustments to crotch depth, thigh, full front thigh, full inner thigh, full buttocks, flat buttocks, protruding tummy, or sway back, the pattern crotch will have changed and you'll need to remeasure.

Refer to the reference points for pattern crotch-length measurements (see the drawing on p. 49). Stand the tape measure on edge and walk it along the center front and back between the waist and crotch point of the pattern. Add the front and back measurements and record the total in column 5 on your Measurement Chart. Determine the difference between columns 4 and 5, and record it in column 6. The difference is the amount of adjustment that should be recorded in column 7. If the pattern is slightly longer, leave it. If you don't have enough crotch length, you will need to add it now. If you wait until you have cut your fabric, you will be in trouble.

When adjusting for the difference, add up to 1 in. at the center-front waist and 1 in.

Crotch Length

If you measured your pattern before you made any adjustments to crotch depth, thigh (front or inner), buttocks, tummy, or sway back, you will now need to remeasure your pattern because your original measurement will have changed.

Refigure the adjustment difference. If the pattern is slightly longer, leave it.

If you need to add more, add up to 1 in. at center front waist and 1 in. at center back waist. Distribute the difference evenly between the two. Remeasure.

If still more is required beyond the maximum that was added above (2 in.), divide the difference between the front and back crotch points.

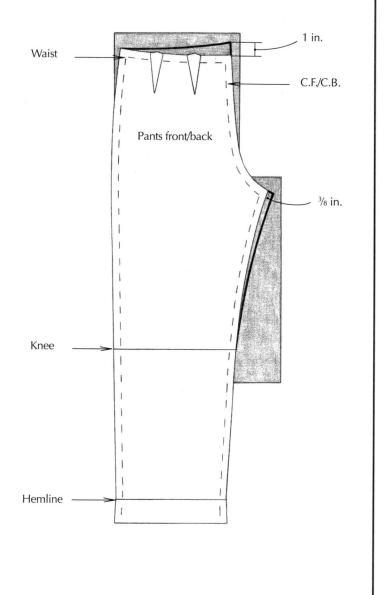

Waist

1 in.

C.F./C.B.

Pants front/back

³⁄₈ in.

Knee

Hemline

at the center-back waist. Distribute the difference evenly between the two. If more length is required than what was added evenly at the center-front and center-back waist, divide the difference between the front and back and add it to each crotch point. For example, if you need to add 2¾ in. to the pattern, add 1 in. at the center front, 1 in. at the center back, ⅜ in. at the front crotch point, and ⅜ in. at the back crotch point.

Truing Your Pattern

Depending on the amount adjusted, the original smooth and continuous pattern lines can be disrupted. Reestablishing or redrawing these lines is called "truing." Check your pattern edges for lines that are no longer continuous curves or straight lines. You'll develop an eye for this with experience. Use a French curve or a styling curve, such as a Fashion Ruler, to achieve the line that best fits your curves.

When reconnecting a line between two points, you may add or subtract small amounts from your pattern above and below the adjustment points when blending this new line. This is normal, but keep it to a minimum. Because of this blending, any fitting subtleties can be worked out in the first fitting. An abrupt change in a line will create a dramatic bulge or hollow when translated into fabric (see the drawing on p. 74).

In addition to some basic tools such as scissors and tape, you will need the following supplies to true your pattern:

- extra paper around your working pattern to allow room for truing (see the photo above)

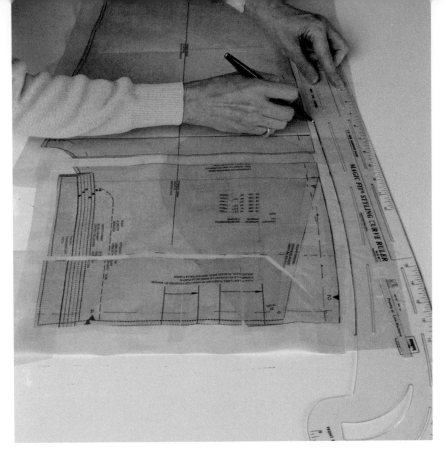

Don't skimp on tissue when you add it to the edge of your pattern. It will make the truing process easier.

- a French curve or Fashion Ruler to true the waist, crotch curve, and inseam from the crotch point to knee line, or anywhere an unbroken curved line is required
- a straightedge to true the side from the hip or thigh line (whichever is larger) to the hemline, from the knee line to the hemline on the inseam, and from the center-front/center-back waist to the beginning of the crotch curve
- a pen, pencil, or fine felt-tip marker

Before you begin to redraw the new pattern edges, review the hints at the top of p. 75.

Three Examples of Truing

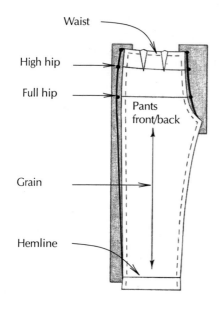

Waist

High hip

Full hip

Pants front/back

Grain

Hemline

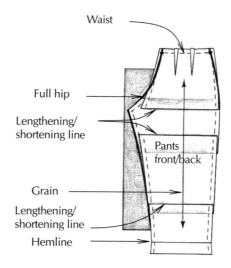

Waist

Full hip

Lengthening/ shortening line

Pants front/back

Grain

Lengthening/ shortening line

Hemline

Where pattern edges have been disrupted by adjustments, redraw the pattern edge so it is a smooth, continuous line.

The bold line is a blended line.

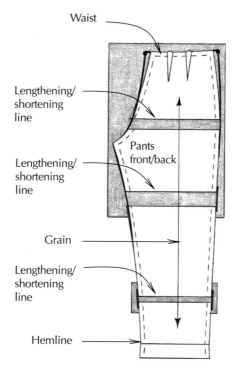

Waist

Lengthening/ shortening line

Lengthening/ shortening line

Pants front/back

Grain

Lengthening/ shortening line

Hemline

- When truing the waist edge, make sure you fold and pin or tape darts or pleats closed (see the photo at right)
- Adjoining seam edges should be the same length. The inseam edge may differ up to ¾ in. due to easing between the knee and the crotch point.
- Match crotch-point seams and make sure there is a smooth continuous line from the center-front waist to the crotch point to the center-back waist. Reblend through the crotch curve if necessary. Do not change the slope of the curve at this time.
- Make sure all pattern pieces are flat. The only exception is when truing the waist edge where darts or pleats must be folded closed.
- If the grainline has been disrupted, redraw it as a straight continuous line.

Fitting the Pattern

Having completed the pattern-adjusting process, you are now ready to move into the final phase of preparing your tissue pattern for fitting. Additional seam allowances will be added just in case additional alteration room is needed when fitting your fabric pants.

Testing the fit

You have several options for testing the fit of your adjusted pattern. You can fit by pinning the pattern together, by making a trial garment, or by altering your fashion-fabric pants.

Pinning the pattern together

You can only use this first method if your pattern has seam allowances included on it. This method is a good, fast choice for easy-to-fit figures or loose styles. Beware, though, that paper patterns are very fragile and easily ripped unless reinforced with tape, especially through the crotch area and upper inseam. By pinning the pattern together you can check basic length and width fit, but it is difficult to measure comfort through movement. Paper doesn't "give," and because you have only half a pattern, crotch length and sitting comfort are hard to determine. Another drawback is trying to visualize the translation from paper to how actual fabric will hang and shape to the body.

If you do pin-fit, first pin all the darts or pleats closed. Reinforce the crotch curve and upper inseam with tape to prevent tearing. Pin the front and back together at the side and inseams. Clip the crotch-curve seam allowance. Turn up a 2-in. hem allowance. Slip the pinned pattern on one leg, matching the center-front, center-back, side, and waist seams to your body.

After you have added extra tissue for truing, fold and pin the waist darts or pleats closed before drawing in a new waistline. When unfolded, the edge of the pattern will be the correct shape.

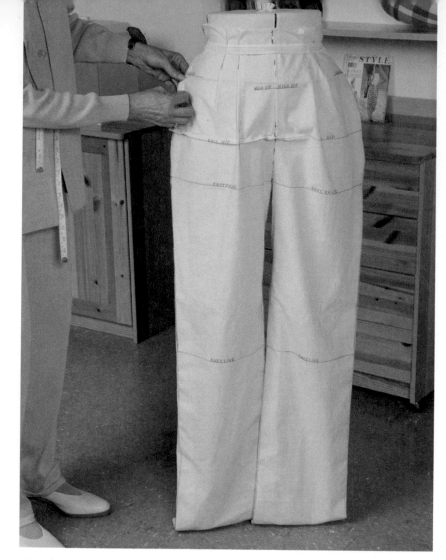

A trial garment made of muslin is a useful fitting tool.

measuring, math, determining ease, or adjusting? If making any new adjustments, make note of the place and amount. Recheck these fitting areas in the fabric pants. Then readjust your Measurement Chart figures.

Making a trial garment Making a trial garment using muslin or an inexpensive fabric similar to what you may choose for a final pair of pants is the second option (see the photo at left). This process is more time-consuming than pin-fitting and is not representative of your actual fabric, but it is a good way to check fit and style and to foolproof several pattern adjustments. Sitting, standing, and movement comfort can be determined. You can also check and recheck fit as many times as necessary, as well as make as many adjustments as needed without concern for the fabric.

Check lengths and widths. Re-pin where necessary if too wide or too long. If the pattern is too small or too short, measure the amount of the needed adjustment. Make adjustments on the pattern. This type of fitting is not intended to get a true fit on close or fitted styles and cannot replace fabric.

Before refiguring adjustment amounts on your Measurement Chart, determine why there is a discrepancy. Did it occur in

Altering your fashion-fabric pants There are several advantages to making your pants in fashion fabric and then checking the fit. First, you can see how your actual fabric looks and drapes. Second, it is easier and faster, especially if you have previously refined your pattern or have few fitting problems. The disadvantages are that some alterations are more difficult and less successful once the fabric is cut out. And making alterations on your fashion fabric may cause the fabric to be overworked. You can damage the fabric, making it

Increasing the seam allowances will permit you to make alterations easily during the construction process.

look worn and old before completion. I do not recommend using this method if using expensive fabric unless you have previously thoroughly proofed the fit of your pattern.

The more you demand, the more figure deviations you have, and the closer the fit, the more reason there is to make a trial garment.

Adding seam allowances

Assuming all measurements, comparisons, and adjustments were made accurately, your garment may still not fit as well as you would like. Although your pants will be statistically correct if you measured and adjusted correctly, it is difficult to account for posture and flesh distribution and how this volume will be taken up in your pants. Therefore, to allow for some alteration room at fabric-fitting time, adjust your seam allowances to the following minimums on the front and back:

- 1 in. on side seams and inseams
- ⅝ in. at the center front, center back, and through the crotch curve
- 2 in. at the waist edges

You may prefer to add any extra seam allowance to your pattern at this time so you don't forget later when cutting out. If you are a more experienced sewer, add the extra on your fabric when you lay out your pattern.

At this point you have completed your major adjustments, determined as closely as possible by measuring both yourself and your pattern. Recheck your measurements and readjust if necessary. You can take fabric out, but you can't add it back in. Further refining of the fit of your pants (fine-tuning small details) will be done early in the fabric-fitting process.

4 Refining the Fit

You are ready to test-fit your adjusted pants pattern in fabric. Only minor changes should be necessary on your fabric pants since major adjustments for measurements were made on your pattern in Chapter 3. Fitting changes made now on your fabric should be transferred to your pattern for a truly personalized custom fit.

Fitting is not an exact science. There is a measure of judgment that only experience can replace. In other words, practice makes perfect, or almost! Whether working with a fitting shell in an inexpensive prototype fabric or fashion fabric you intend to wear, the alteration and adjustment process is done by first pin fitting the fabric on your body, then transferring these alterations through measurements to your pattern and adjusting it. The difficult part is knowing how to transfer these adjustments, when you should make them, and where on the paper pattern to make them.

Pants are a complex problem of translation from a two-dimensional pattern to a three-dimensional garment. Because volume can change the curves and shape of your pants the fit is also affected. Is that 40-in. circumference round, elliptical, oval, more heart shaped, or square?

When fitting your pants, keep in mind the style of the pattern you have chosen. Don't try to transform a loose-fitting trouser style into a jeans fit. The two styles are designed differently from the start. They each fit differently because the purpose and activities each are worn for are very different.

Analyzing the Fit

Use the illustration on the facing page when analyzing the fit of your pants. Differences will help you determine what refining alterations may be necessary. Check the fit while standing and sitting. Crotch length can vary depending on personal comfort. You should be able to pinch about ½ in. of fabric at the crotch and inseam intersection. Side seams should hang straight down the sides of the legs from the waist to the hemline. There should be sufficient ease at the full hip so you can pinch 2 in. to 3 in. of fabric at the sides (less for slacks). Leg width will vary with hip width. Pants that are too wide can look too large, and too tapered a leg can emphasize the hips.

Why You May Need to Refine the Fit

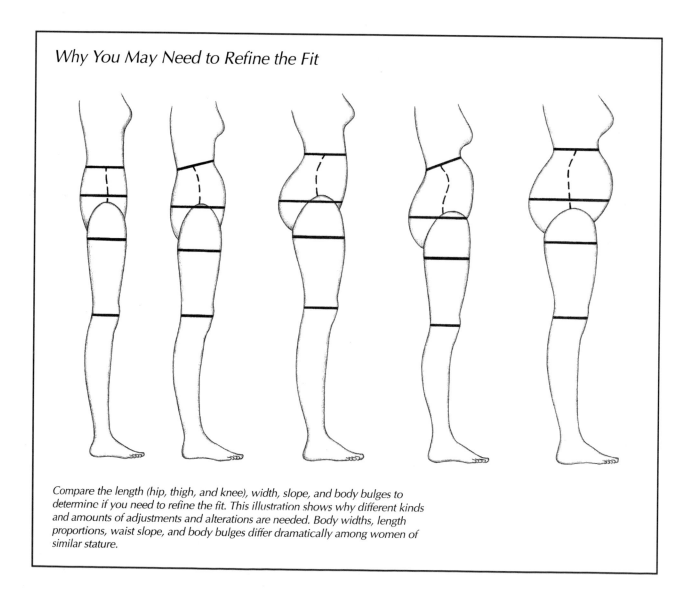

Compare the length (hip, thigh, and knee), width, slope, and body bulges to determine if you need to refine the fit. This illustration shows why different kinds and amounts of adjustments and alterations are needed. Body widths, length proportions, waist slope, and body bulges differ dramatically among women of similar stature.

If you've worked accurately to this point, refining your fit should involve small, subtle changes. Although these changes may seem minor, they are personal changes due to posture, bone structure, or flesh distribution, not style. Some of these changes may be a matter of personal preference rather than a fitting problem. Enlist the assistance of someone else to help in this nip-and-tuck process. Any slight bending or twisting can result in wrinkles, giving you a false sense of the need to adjust. Your pants may look fine to the observer but feel uncomfortable to you.

Some fabrics feel differently, drape differently, and allow a different amount of ease than others. One pair of pants using the same pattern but different fabric than another pair may require some minor changes. For example, on my basic pattern I have two back crotch curves marked, one higher, one lower. When cutting out, I use the higher crotch curve, knowing that when I get the waistband on, I can sew the crotch lower if the fit is too close to my body or if it feels uncomfortable. The two front pleats are made larger or transformed into three when I make my pants in silk instead of wool. Because the bulkiness and draping qualities of fabric differ,

slightly varying the fit, these small changes are not uncommon when fitting your fashion fabric pants.

Small decreases or increases can make a noticeable difference, so work in small increments of ¼ in. for each alteration. Do one alteration at a time. If you notice improvement, it worked!

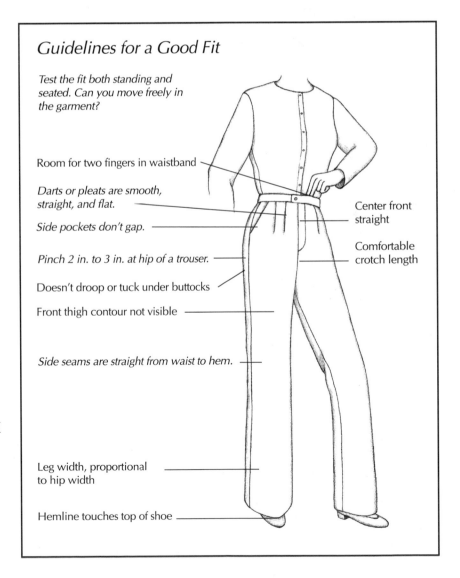

Guidelines for a Good Fit

Test the fit both standing and seated. Can you move freely in the garment?

Room for two fingers in waistband

Darts or pleats are smooth, straight, and flat.

Side pockets don't gap.

Pinch 2 in. to 3 in. at hip of a trouser.

Doesn't droop or tuck under buttocks

Front thigh contour not visible

Side seams are straight from waist to hem.

Leg width, proportional to hip width

Hemline touches top of shoe

Center front straight

Comfortable crotch length

During the refining process, use different color pens for each fitting to record the amount of change on your Measurement Chart and when making pattern adjustments. That way you can easily identify what changes and the amounts that were made at each fitting. You will end up with a final fit list of adjustments that should be a compilation of your original pattern adjustments and fabric pant alterations. This will be your adjustment guide on future commercial patterns.

Adding the Third Dimension

You've measured, compared, and adjusted your pattern so it is a two-dimensional statistical representation of your body—leaving no guesswork. Now it's time to add the third dimension: volume. Don't automatically assume that your adjusted pattern is going to be a perfect fit. The next step is to test your adjustments in fabric. As I recommended, if you made your pants out of an inexpensive fabric you can mark on it, pin and sew out unnecessary fabric if the pants are too loose, and sew in additional fabric pieces if an area is too snug, too short, or has an insufficient seam allowance. You can try the pants on as many times as necessary to achieve your perfect fit.

Factors that affect fit

When fitting your pants there are several factors that affect their fit and feel. These include posture, heel height, undergarments, panty hose, and time of day or month. Try to replicate these factors so that your fabric fitting will be an exact representation of when your measurements were taken. For every fitting problem there can be several solutions. Likewise,

one solution can fix several problems. Don't try and make too many corrections for the same problem at once until you know whether or not there has been improvement.

Fitting order

In order to fit your fabric pants keep construction as simple as possible by pinning or basting the front and back together. For the sake of comfort when testing movement and sitting room, I suggest basting the front and back together at the center, crotch, and inseams. Eliminate the zipper at this time but leave an opening to get into your pants. Pockets do not need to be incorporated unless they complete the pants front, such as the underlay of slant pockets. Fit first without the waistband. Refer to Fitting Your Pants during Construction (p. 93) for more hints and guidelines when constructing your fashion fabric pants or prototype.

It is best to do fitting in a logical sequence. To avoid over fitting and disrupting the lay of the pleats, pin or baste them down. Begin at the waist and gradually dissipate pleat take-up as you near the crotch level or as pinned on your pattern when

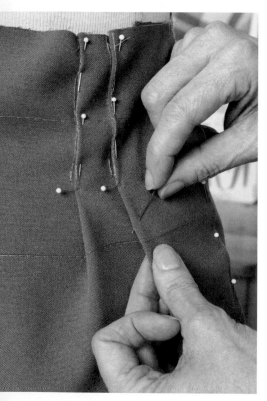

Pin pleats down to where you want the fullness to disperse before checking the fit.

Fitting Waist, Hip, and Thigh Areas

Assess the looseness or tightness of fit in the width areas of your pants.

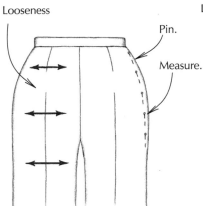

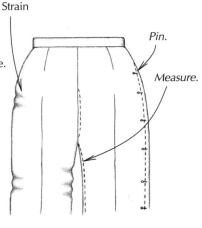

Looseness   Pin.   Measure.

Decrease

Looseness   Pin.   Measure.

Increase

Strain   Pin.   Measure.

If your pants are too loose in the waist, high hip, or full hip, pin out the excess at the sides. If the leg is too wide in the thigh area and below, pin out the excess at the side and inseam. If too tight, release the side seams through the waist and hip areas until your pants are comfortable or there are no more horizontal wrinkles evident. Release the side seam and inseam for thigh and leg.

*Measure the excess pinned out or the amounts released at both side seams on front and back waist and hip areas to determine the **total** decrease or increase amount. Divide this new alteration amount by 4 if it's 2 in. or less, or by 8 if it's more than 2 in. Decrease or increase front and back pattern pieces this new amount (as instructed in Chapter 3) for waist and hips.*

*For thigh and leg, measure the amount of the decrease or increase at the side and inseam front and back to determine the **total** amount of change. Divide this new total by 4. Decrease or increase front and back pattern pieces as instructed in Chapter 3 for thigh increase/decrease.*

you measured it. Then follow this step-by-step fitting sequence.

1. Assess whether the waist and hip area is too big or too small (see the drawing above). Take in or let out as necessary on each side to achieve a comfortable,

balanced, stress-free fit. Don't worry about the darts right now. Do not adjust your pattern yet.

2. Arrange the pants so the full hip line is parallel to the floor in front and back.

3. Fasten a 1-in. elastic band or Ban-Rol at the same waist level as when measured.

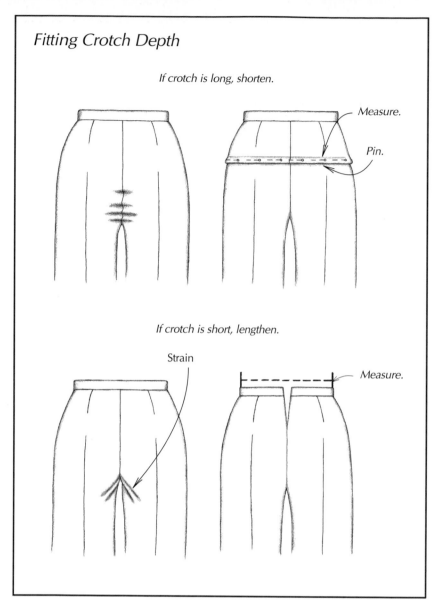

Fitting Crotch Depth

If crotch is long, shorten.

Measure.

Pin.

If crotch is short, lengthen.

Strain

Measure.

4. Check length proportions beginning with the crotch depth. The intersection of the crotch and inseam should be ½ in. to 1 in. below your body. If too long, pin out the excess as in the drawing above, below the waist but above the crotch line level. If too short, lengthen by dropping the waist. Measure the

amount shortened or lengthened and adjust your pattern to reflect these alterations. Refigure the adjustment amount in column 7 on your Measurement Chart. Next check the waist to knee proportion. The knee line mark on your fabric should closely match the front middle of your knee. Pin out the excess if too long, parallel to the floor, between the crotch line and knee line. If too short, measure the distance between the knee line marking on your fabric and your actual mid-knee. Measure the amount to be shortened or lengthened. Adjust your pattern. Refigure the adjustment amount in column 7 as for crotch depth.

5. You did a general too big or too small adjustment in step 1 so your pants wouldn't fall off or ride too high. Now refine the circumference fit of the waist, high hip, full hip, and thigh. This may involve taking in or letting out different amounts in each of these areas. It may also be necessary to rebalance the side seams in these fitting areas, especially the waist and high hip. This means that if your front or back half is proportionally larger in any of these areas, you may need to let out or take in different amounts on the front and back seams so the side seam will hang straight and not curve to the front or back where more fabric is needed due to a body bulge. You are contouring the fit to your body, so take in or let out on the side and inseams to achieve the fit and comfort, as well as the personal style, you prefer. Alter leg width from knee line to hem equally at the side and inseam. Measure altered amounts in these areas. Adjust your pattern, then refigure the adjustment amount in column 7 on your Measurement Chart.

6. Fit the waistband, altering the pleats or darts as needed. Refining them will be done later.

7. Crotch length can be increased or decreased at the center front or back by raising or lowering the waist seam. More specific alterations for excess fullness or tightness in the front or back upper thigh and buttocks can be made by lengthening or shortening the crotch point (see the top drawing at right). Measure the alteration amounts. Adjust your pattern and refigure the adjustment amount in column 7 of your Measurement Chart.

Altering the crotch curve on the front or back may require changing the slope or angle of the curve to fit more comfortably and to reduce wrinkling (see the bottom drawing at right). A bit of testing is required here, so make alterations in small amounts—¼ in. or less each time. The seam allowance will be trimmed later to ¼ in., which will give a slightly looser fit.

8. Refine the darts.

9. Alter the finished length.

Fitting Crotch Length

Decrease

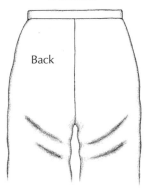

Increase

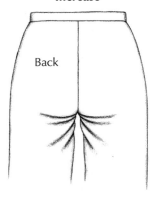

If pants sag and wrinkle under the buttocks, reduce the crotch length on the back only. Decreases should be made:
- *at crotch point on inseam for a flat buttocks*

OR
- *at waist for a flat buttocks*

Increases should be made:
- *at crotch point on inseam if fabric cups under buttocks*
- *at waist for full buttocks*

Altering Crotch Curve

May be done on front, back, or both according to need and comfort.

Raise crotch curve

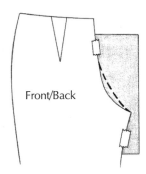

Lower crotch curve

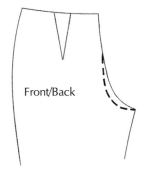

The crotch curve needs to be raised when you have one of the following:
- *Low full abdomen*
- *Prominent pubic bone*
- *High and/or full buttocks*

The crotch curve needs to be lowered when you have one of the following:
- *Excess fabric just above crotch at pubic bone*
- *Low buttocks*
- *Back crotch seam cutting between buttocks*

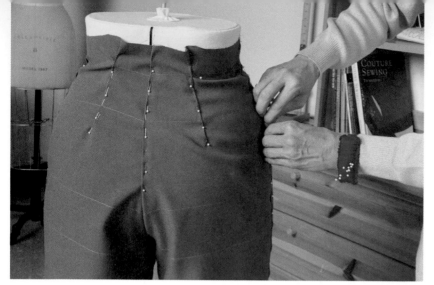

Horizontal wrinkles indicate that the pants are too tight in the high hip area while the diamond-shaped wrinkle in the seat area indicates that the center back seam is too angled and the crotch curve too shallow.

Read your wrinkles (on your pants)!

Vertical wrinkles mean pants are too loose. Horizontal or diagonal wrinkles mean pants are too tight someplace (see the photos at left). This could involve one alteration or several in different places.

Guidelines for darts and pleats

Although pleat size is specified on the pattern, the size and number of pleats can be increased or decreased to help fit the waist. The size, number, shape, length, and angle of generic pattern darts can be modified so your fabric is contoured like your body. Darts are one of the most important ways to achieve fit. Darts closest to the side seam are usually shorter and shape the hip curve while darts closest to center front or back provide shaping for tummies and buttocks. If your waist is the same size or larger than your hips, you may not need any darts. A pattern adjustment made in Chapter 3 for crotch depth may signal the need for a dart length alteration. You may need to make some changes to the pleats and darts or to combine these changes with seam alterations to achieve a well-contoured fit. Here are some guidelines for specific problems.

Postural variation can cause diagonal wrinkles at the back of the leg. Eliminate them by decreasing the length of the back leg above the knee line. Increase the length the same amount below the knee line to keep vertical seams the same length as front.

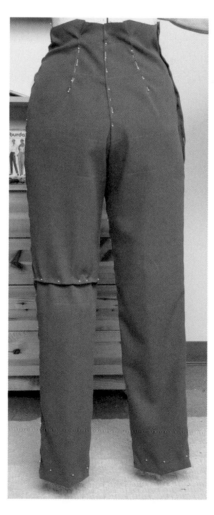

Fleshy round high hip A fleshy round hip will require a larger dart. Increase the size of the dart closest to the side seam to give a more rounded effect just below the point. Redraw the dart with an inward curve to allow for greater fullness in the high-hip area. A pleat or side seam alteration may be necessary to compensate for the slight reduction in waist size.

Flat or concave high hip This dart alteration requires a smaller dart closest to the side seam to reduce the bulge just below the dart point because the body is less curved. Increase pleats or side seams to take up additional waist increase created by reducing the dart size. Redraw the dart with an outward curve to take out extra fabric fullness created by a flatter body.

Full or flat buttocks To create more room for full buttocks, increase the dart closest to the center back. For flat buttocks, less room is required so decrease the dart closest to center back.

Angle of darts To create a slimmer look while still doing the same fitting, try angling the back dart(s) parallel to the side seam or center back (see the drawing below). If you change the angle, the dart must still point to the area where the fullness is needed. Reangle the back dart if you changed the angle of the center back seam.

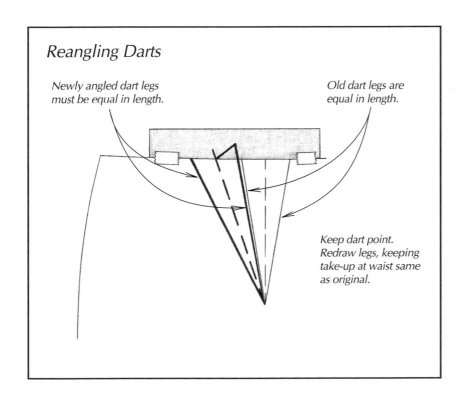

Reangling Darts

Newly angled dart legs must be equal in length.

Old dart legs are equal in length.

Keep dart point. Redraw legs, keeping take-up at waist same as original.

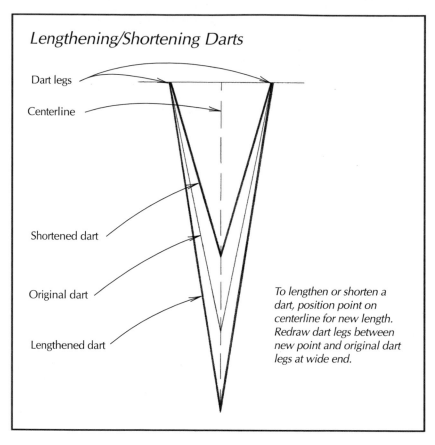

Lengthening/Shortening Darts

Dart legs

Centerline

Shortened dart

Original dart

Lengthened dart

To lengthen or shorten a dart, position point on centerline for new length. Redraw dart legs between new point and original dart legs at wide end.

Reshaping Darts

Reshape straight darts to provide more or less room over a body curve.

New dart drawn with inward curve (1/16 in. to 1/8 in.)

New dart drawn with outward curve (1/16 in. to 1/8 in.)

New dart leg stitching lines

Excess fabric at end of dart

The problem can be solved by shortening the dart (see the top drawing at left), by decreasing its size, or by reshaping the dart (see the bottom drawing at left). You may need to do all three. If excess fabric still remains, make two smaller darts that total the same width at the wide end as the original single dart.

Excess fabric in the dart area

Eliminate this problem by increasing the size of the dart, by reshaping the dart, or by lengthening the dart (see the top drawing at left). Sometimes you must apply a combination of these solutions, do all three, or make two smaller darts. For a better fit if you have a sway back, try curving the wide end of the dart outward then gradually curving it inward toward the point.

Your Permanent Pattern

Now that you have fine-tuned the fit of your pants, check to make sure you have transferred all alterations on your fabric pants to adjustments on your pattern. Column 7 on your Measurement Chart should also reflect these changes. For future reference, make notes on your chart regarding crotch curve alterations as well as what pleats and darts you have changed and how. Your adjusted tissue pattern should now accurately represent

Make a permanent pattern by tracing your working pattern onto sturdy see-through material, drawing in all reference points and pattern markings.

the fit of your pants. This pattern can be used to make many pairs of pants, and you'll save a lot of time not having to fit them all. You will also be able to adjust a new commercial pattern based on your revised adjustment record or to apply adjustments to ready-to-wear pants to get a better fit. Keep in mind, though, that not all adjustments are possible once pants are constructed.

You can also use your adjusted pattern to design new style variations. (See Chapter 6 for more on stylizing your pants.)

Once your working pattern is finalized you want to make sure that your pattern will last. Make a clean copy, without all the tape and added paper. There are specific products for this purpose. They are available in paper, nonwoven material, and plastic and come with various size preprinted grids or plain. I do not recommend fusing your working tissue pattern to more permanent material. If you have used tape, you can end up with a gooey mess on your iron and a ruined pattern. Copy all the grainlines and pattern markings. Indicate all the horizontal length lines such as high hip, full hip, crotchline, kneeline, and hemline. Record the date, your weight, and the pattern name, number, and size.

5 Constructing the Pants

You've worked meticulously on preparing and adjusting your pattern to get the perfect fit. Careless fabric preparation or rushed construction can be the cause of poor fit just as much as figure deviations. Each step of the construction process is as important as measuring, adjusting, and altering. Fitting is a continual refining process progressing through construction.

Methods of practical fitting vary greatly. Your objective is to get a picture of the whole situation and assess the fit of your pants as quickly as possible. Fit is affected by the behavior of your fabric. As with the pattern adjusting you did in Chapter 3, fitting is a systematic, sequential process. Whether you jump directly into the permanent construction of your pants or you progressively fit during construction will depend on whether or not you have tested the fit of your pattern. The degree of fit demanded by the style of your pattern also plays an important role in your decision. Unless you have used this pattern before and proofed the fit in an actual garment, I advise first doing some basic, structural-seams-only construction to validate this picture to avoid later ripping out your permanent stitching to make alterations. Pin or base the side, inseams, center front, and back crotch seams to get a general feel for the fit of your pants. Try your pants on. Based on what you see and how your pants feel, you can determine if you need to refine your fit or can immediately begin the permanent stitching and construction of your pants.

I recommend that you resist the temptation to make any further pattern changes other than those that accompany the fitting alterations. You've done the hard part. Now enjoy sewing.

Constructing Fashion Fabric Pants

Fabric that is pattern ready has been trued, preshrunk, and pressed. Whether working with a prototype or actual fashion fabric, accuracy in cutting, marking, and sewing can affect the fit and the look of your pants. I've listed the general steps for constructing pants to give you an overview of the sewing process. More detailed instructions for each step will follow later in the chapter. I advise consulting your pattern guide sheet sewing instructions because details and processes within differently styled pants can vary. Therefore, the construction order for your pants may be slightly different.

1. Cut the prototype or fashion fabric. Wait to cut the lining until after alterations on the fabric are completed and transferred to the pattern. This saves time so the lining doesn't have to be recut due to fitting alterations.

2. Transfer construction markings, darts, and pleats to the fabric.

3. Sew the darts and pleats.

4. Press the darts and/or pleats.

5. Apply the pockets.

6. Install the zipper.

7. Sew the inseams.

8. Sew the side seams.

9. Stitch the crotch seam.

10. Fit and mark the waistline if not previously done. Fit the waistband.

11. Baste the lining to the pants at the waist edge.

12. Attach the waistband, belt loops, casing, or waist facing (whichever applies).

13. Sew a hook and bar or button and buttonhole on the waistband.

14. Hem and/or cuff the pants. For a prototype, simply pin the hem.

For lining, follow the general construction steps 1 through 4, 7 through 9, 11, and 14. Leave the lining seam open above the zipper installation. For a fly zipper, see p. 114 for special lining preparation.

Fitting Your Pants during Construction

The following guidelines will help you fit your pants throughout the construction process, just in case minor adjustments need to made. These can apply whether you are using a fashion fabric or a prototype fabric.

- Use a contrasting color thread when basting your seams.
- If this is the first time you have used your pattern, pin or baste the inseam and side seams for easiest adjusting and baste the ⅝-in. crotch seam, leaving an opening at the front or back for trying on the pants (see the photo at right). Pin the opening closed on the seamline.
- Eliminate all details such as pockets and zippers. These are added later once you are sure of the fit.
- Cut the waistband 6 in. longer than your waist body measurement (column 1 on your Measurement Chart), and 3¾ in. wide for a 1¼-in. finished band.
- If working with a prototype fabric for fitting only, mark all personal pattern reference points on the outside of the fabric as well as seamlines so you can pinpoint the location and amounts of alteration/ adjustment needed.

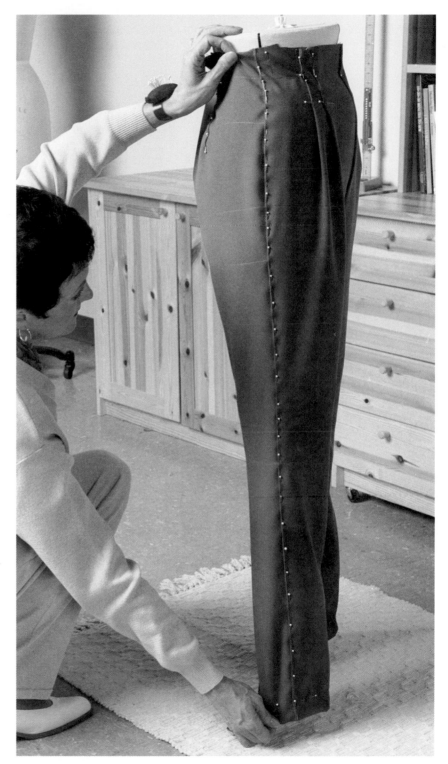

Pin-basting the side seams and inseams is a quick way to check your fit and make alterations before the final sewing.

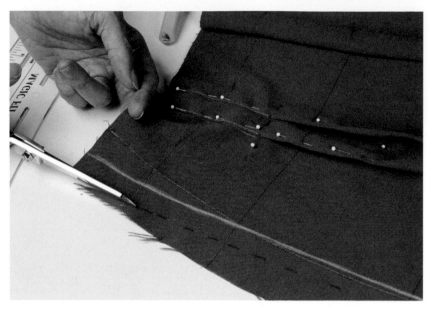

Recut your seam allowances to an even width after you've made your alterations.

Layout, Cutting, and Marking

Many sewers, motivated to see their pants sewn together, hurry through the layout, cutting, and marking process thinking the sewing process is the most important. Nothing can be more misleading. Accuracy and precision begins now with laying out your pattern and proceeds through the cutting and marking. Working carefully now will result in a better-looking and better-fitting pair of pants. Careful preparation of your fabric for the sewing process is time well spent.

Layout

If your pattern does not have seam allowances included, add them in now. Add a minimum of 1 in. to side seams and inseams and 2 in. above the horizontal waistline on the front and back and ⅝ in. to the center crotch seams. If your pattern has seam allowances included, add enough to total 1 in. on side seams and inseams and 2 in. above the horizontal waistline. This will allow some extra alteration room and can always be trimmed.

On the first page of your pattern guide sheet you will see various cutting diagrams. The pattern is laid on the fabric in these layouts in a particular way. Choose the layout that corresponds to the

- If working with fashion fabric, use a marking procedure that can be easily seen and removed but does not rub off or harm the surface of your fabric.
- Before removing the pins or basting stitches, mark the seamline, making sure all seam allowances are an even width to avoid construction confusion and later misfits.
- Consult the sewing instructions on your pattern guide sheet and the construction sequence specific to your pattern details.

pattern view, size, and fabric width you are using. If you are lining your pants, the lining fabric may be a different width than your pants fabric. If so, a different cutting layout will be used to correspond to your fabric width. Fold the fabric with the wrong sides out and selvages together or as diagrammed in the cutting layout. Usually fabric will be folded along the length, parallel to the selvage. Whenever possible, place pattern pieces going in the same up/down direction. Some fabrics absorb or reflect light differently when viewed from opposite directions (top to bottom vs. bottom to top). A color difference may be noticeable when worn if the pattern pieces are not laid out in the same direction.

Place the pants front and back on the fabric first. Next position the pattern pieces that require a folded fabric edge followed by any remaining pieces. If possible, reserve space along a single selvage to cut the waistband. For pieces that are marked with a grainline arrow, place a pin at one end of the grainline arrow. Measure between the pin and selvage or fold. Pivot the other end of the grainline arrow until it measures the same distance, then pin. Use pins or weights to secure the pattern to the fabric. Precisely measure each piece to ensure straight grain placement.

Cutting doesn't have to be a chore with the right equipment and comfortable table height.

Cutting

As you begin to cut your fabric, here are some suggestions from my experience that help me cut accurately and prevent fabric distortion.

- Handle your fabric as little as possible to prevent stretching.
- Use sharp shears with a bent handle. They allow you to keep the pattern and fabric flat on the solid cutting surface. Do not lift the shears off the cutting surface, and take long, even strokes.
- Hold the fabric down flat with your free hand close to the edge of the pattern to prevent slippage. Use long, firm strokes on straight edges and shortened strokes around curves. A rotary cutter and mat can be used instead of shears.

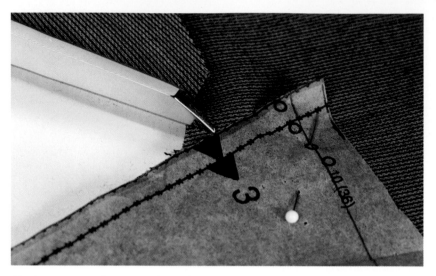

Cutting out notches away from the pattern provides more seam allowance room for alterations.

- Cut multiple notches as one. If there isn't room to cut the notches out, designate their position by marking with tracing paper. I prefer cutting notches "out," away from the pattern until I'm sure of the fit (see the photo above). Cutting notches this way is important if you only have ⅝-in. seam allowances. If you cut the V-shaped notch in toward your pattern, you reduce the size of the seam allowance. You compromise the usable amount of seam allowance for alteration purposes if your pattern fit was not previously proofed, as well as the amount left for finishing your seams. If the notch is cut out, away from the pattern, the next time you use it you can mark the notches with a small snip in the edge of the fabric.

Marking

Pattern symbols are your road map through construction, so marking correctly is essential. Marking is done after the fabric is cut out but before the pattern pieces are removed.

Construction symbols to be marked include dots, stitching lines (such as topstitching line for fly zipper), foldlines, center front line for fly zipper, darts, tucks, pleats, buttonhole(s), and pocket placement lines.

The methods and tools you use to mark depend on your fabric, the pattern symbol, and which side of the fabric that needs to be marked. You can choose from a variety of methods to mark your fabric. The most common are tracing, pin marking, tailor tacks, or baste marking with contrasting thread. Some pattern marking may require two different marking methods and tools to transfer construction marks to your fabric. Most marking is done on the wrong side. Pleats, topstitching, and pocket placement lines can be the exception. Some of the tools you may need include the following:

- Tracing paper and tracing wheel (choose the lightest color paper that is visible on your fabric)
- Dressmaker's pencil or tailor's chalk
- Fabric marking pen that is air erasable and water soluble

To mark fabric with a tracing wheel, place tracing paper against the wrong side of the fabric and run the wheel along the pattern markings.

Clear and accurate markings will make your sewing easier.

MARKING HINTS

Regardless of the method and tools you use, the marking method should be readily visible, accurate, and easily removed (or not visible) on the right side of your fabric. Here are some hints.

• Always do a test on both right and wrong sides of the fabric to check for visibility and ease of removal.

• Use a straightedge or French curve for accuracy in marking lines and curves.

• For long lines, mark dots along the line, then connect the marks with chalk, fabric marking pen, or dressmaker's pencil.

• For lines on the right side of the fabric, first mark the line on the wrong side with dressmaker's tracing paper. Then baste on the line to mark the right side (see the photo at right).

• If it is difficult to tell the right side of the fabric from the wrong side, mark the wrong side with a piece of removable tape.

• If the garment piece will be interfaced, mark it after applying the interfacing.

• During construction keep pattern pieces handy for quick reference of pattern markings.

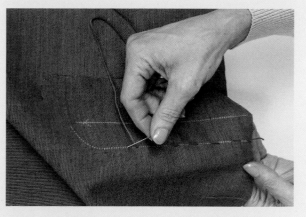

To mark on the right side, baste from the wrong side in a contrasting color.

Lining Your Pants

If you decide to line your pants, the following guidelines will help you get the best results.

- Line only the knee area 5 in. above and below the knee line to prevent baggy knees.
- Lay out, cut, and mark the lining in the same way you did the fashion fabric. Attention to one-direction placement of pieces is not necessary.
- Cut the lining on the crosswise grain (if pattern length permits) to help prevent the pants from stretching.
- If you know the exact finished length of your pants, cut the lining ½ in. longer at this time, or wait and determine the length at the time of hemming.
- Stitch darts and pleats in the lining. When pressing, lay darts in the opposite direction from the fashion fabric to reduce bulk.
- Increase seam allowances by ¹⁄₁₆ in. Sew, finish (if necessary), and press side seams and inseams, leaving the zipper area open.
- Reduce the seam allowance through the crotch curve to ½ in. so the lining doesn't "sit" on top of the fashion fabric.

Pressing

There are a variety of pressing tools available. Some are basic tools used generally for all types of garment construction. Others are helpful for specific garments or fabrics.

Basic tools

- Tailor's ham for maintaining the shaping of curved seams and darts
- Seam roll

Besides general pressing tools, use seamstick, brown paper, and needle board for special pressing problems.

- Sleeve board
- Point presser/clapper
- See-through press cloth for nonwool fabrics
- Steam/dry iron
- Padded table or board

Special helpful tools

- Padded seam stick for pressing leg seams open (substitute a heavy cardboard tube in a pinch)
- Needle or Velvaboard for napped fabrics
- Two strips of brown paper that are 2 in. wide and as long as possible to use under seams and darts to prevent the outline from showing on the right side of the fabric, especially on plain dark fabrics and gabardines
- A large press cloth about 15 in. by 30 in. My favorite is fine muslin and ivory wool challis washed several times and sewn together so it is 15 in. by 60 in.

Techniques

Good pressing throughout construction is as important as sewing straight seams. It is the key to a custom-made look. Maintaining the grain and texture of your fabric as well as shaping it to your body contours assures you of a neat, professional-looking pair of pants.

- Before beginning a project, make up several seam samples and do a test run, varying the iron temperature setting and moisture slightly. See what gives you the best results.
- Press with the grain of the fabric.
- Because you will be pressing during construction, use an up-and-down motion rather than a gliding motion as in ironing.
- Press as you go. Every time the sewing machine touches my fabric I press, even if only to smooth staystitching or basting.
- Make sure you are satisfied with the fit before pressing darts, pleats, or seams.
- After sewing a seam, lay your pants flat and press over the line of stitching. This embeds the stitches into the fabric and smooths the seam before further processing.
- Generally, press seam allowances open and flat unless doing a special type of seam or finish.
- Do not press over pins or basting thread (unless using silk thread).
- Allow fabric to dry thoroughly before handling.
- Press after completing seam finishes or special seams.
- Press on the wrong side.
- Use a press cloth when top pressing.
- Use a ham to shape and smooth darts and to press curved seams.
- If using a napped fabric, always lay the right side against the needle or Velvaboard.

Seams and Finishes

Plain seams are the backbone of garment construction and are the seams most often illustrated in your pattern guide sheet sewing instructions. Plain seams can require some special handling or finishing and are an essential part of the sewing process. Your pants' durability and appearance are a result of smooth, well-finished seams. When making a choice about which seam finish to use, consider the type of fabric, style and purpose of your pants, sewing equipment you have available, and your time and sewing experience.

Plain seams

A plain seam is the most common way of joining two pieces of fabric. Many other seams and finishes are derived from it. The edges of the seam allowance are left exposed on the inside of the garment. The edges may be finished to make them more durable or to reduce bulk. Standards for a plain seam are as follows:

- Stitching secured at each end
- Even and accurate seam allowances
- Flat and smooth
- Free of distortion
- Pressed open and flat

Seam finishes

Seam finishes provide a neat edge and prevent raveling, distortion, or the seam from pulling out. Seams can be stitched and pinked, double stitched and trimmed, serged or overlocked, or bound. Choose the finish that works best with the fabric you have chosen, taking into consideration how much the fabric ravels, how much it will be laundered, bulk, and how much time you have to complete your project. Points to keep in mind when selecting the finish are:

- Location of the seam
- Whether your pants are lined
- Whether your pants will be laundered or dry-cleaned

Creaseline

Classic pleated-trouser-style pants generally have a pressed-in creaseline, which can be established before construction is started. The front creaseline extends from the hem into the first pleat. The procedure is simple: Fold each front pants leg in half right side out, matching the side seam to the inseam at the hem to establish the midpoint. For darted pants the front creaseline begins 3 in. above crotch level and extends to the hem. The back creaseline extends from the midpoint at the hem edge to the crotch level.

It is more difficult to remove and reestablish the creaseline after your pants are completed. Therefore you should be completely satisfied with the fit and leg width before establishing the creaseline. Any alteration after the creaseline is set could distort it so it would not be centered on the leg.

Darts and Pleats

Darts and pleats don't present any challenge in the cutting process. Their symmetry in length and width depends on precise marking and sewing.

Darts

Darts shape straight fabric to fit the curved areas of the figure. They widen at the waist where the fabric width needs to be reduced and taper to a point in the hip area where fabric width needs to be increased. Darts vary in size and shape. It is not unusual to have two darts on the front or back of your pattern, each one a different size and length. Each one is positioned to fit a different curve of the body.

Directions and marking Darts are constructed on the wrong side of the fabric. To make it easier to match the stitching lines at the wide end, make a small clip in the edge of the fabric on each marked stitching line. Chalk in a ½-in. line

If you are sure of the fit, press the creaseline in before construction.

perpendicular to the point of the dart. This ensures that there will be no guessing about the exact end point.

Procedure Fold each dart carefully, matching lines and pin. Begin stitching at the wide end and continue to the point, which is marked by the perpendicular line. Stop at the point with your needle in your fabric and on the edge of the fold. To eliminate a bulge at the dart point, shorten your stitch length to 1 or to 18 to 20 stitches per inch. Take four stitches beyond the marked end line. Stitches should be right along the fold edge (see the left photo on the facing page). Run the last stitch off the fold. Tie several square knots at the point to secure. Clip threads ½ in. from the knot. Press the dart flat as stitched, being careful not to press a crease in beyond the point. Then shape over a ham and press the dart from the wrong side. Darts are usually pressed with the folded edge lying toward the center front or back.

Pleats

Pleats are folds of fabric providing controlled fullness where you want it. Pleats can be stitched down, crisply pressed, or softly released. The type of fabric you're using will determine whether your pleats are intended to be crisp and sharp or soft and gentle. Pleats work best on light- to medium-weight fabrics. Pleats on heavyweight fabrics tend to be too bulky. A crisp edge can be attained with linen, poplin, flannel, gabardine, crepe de chine, lightweight wool, broad-cloth, or similar fabrics. In some fabrics, a burst of steam without touching the iron to the fabric is sufficient. For a soft look, a delicate touch with the iron is important, or you can allow the pleats to flow without pressing.

Marking and direction
Transfer pleat line markings to the right side of fabric. Experiment now to see which direction you want your pleats to face: center or side. Try them one way on one side and the opposite way on the other side.

Procedure On the right side of the fabric, crease the foldline or leading edge and bring it over in the direction marked on the tissue pattern to meet the placement line (the line the directional arrow points to). Make sure pleat lines are parallel and all edges are perfectly even at the waist edge. Pin in place. Machine-baste at ½ in. and ¾ in. through the double thickness parallel to the waist edge, or machine-stitch (edgestitch) close to the fold edge if desired (see the right photo on the facing page).

Pockets

No matter what type of pockets your pants have—patch, inserted, or welt—there are some steps you can take to help your pockets hold their shape, look crisp, and contour to your body. First, you should stabilize the pants or pocket by fusing a ¾-in. strip of interfacing over the seamline in the stitching area where the pocket is to be attached. To help prevent stretching, cut the joining edge of an angled pocket on the straight grain or selvage. During application, sew in a ¼-in.-wide piece of stay tape, lining selvage, or silk/polyester ribbon to help maintain shaping. Use a tailor's

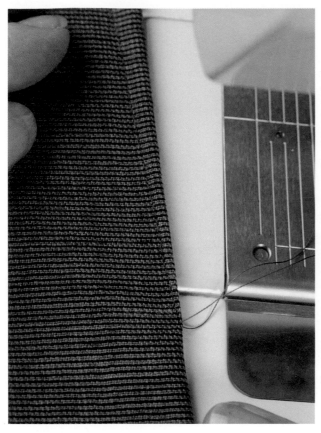

A well-sewn dart is smooth and even all the way down. The chalk mark ensures that darts are the same length.

Baste pleats down twice so they won't shift or become distorted.

ham when pressing slant or inseam inserted pockets to maintain the hip curve shaping. A clapper will help to flatten any bulk. Whenever possible, understitch (as you would a facing) pocket seams where they attach to your pants to help keep edges flat and the seam from rolling to the outside.

The most common type of pocket in pants is an inseam pocket. This style of pocket is inserted in the side seam, and the pocket sack is hidden inside the pants. It is inconspicuous and the easiest to sew for a beginner. Typically this type of pocket is an extension of the pants and is cut all in one with the pants front and back. However, as an alternate method, some patterns have you cut the pocket as a separate piece. The pocket is cut four times, two times on double-thickness fabric for each pocket in the pants. One pocket piece is stitched to each pants front and back. This is a little more time-consuming than the pocket that is included as part of the main pattern pieces and cut as one.

If your pattern includes either type of inseam side pocket, your pattern guide sheet will instruct you how to sew and finish them. I prefer side-seam pockets that are caught in the horizontal waist seam as opposed to pockets that are cut as separate pieces and attached only to each front and back side seam. Pockets attached at the waist are supported by this seam, preventing them from dragging and distorting the side seams. This is especially important if your pockets are used for something other than decorative purposes.

Pocket instructions/ procedure

To make inseam pockets or convert ones that are not sewn at the waist, follow these steps.

1. If you have a dart or pleat in the area that will be covered by the pocket, pin it closed.

2. Place a 15-in. by 8-in. piece of see-through paper over your pants side front and secure with tape or pins. Trace the side edge of the pattern from the waist down $9\frac{1}{2}$ in. Mark two points along this side line, one $1\frac{1}{2}$ in. from the waist and the second $7\frac{1}{2}$ in. from the waist. These marks designate the pocket opening. From the side waist, mark a point 3 in. in toward the center front along the waist edge. The pocket will be 11 in.

at its deepest point and $6\frac{1}{2}$ in. at its widest point. Draw in a completed pocket line beginning at the lowest side mark, sloping down to the lowest point of the pocket, around to the widest, and finishing at the waist mark. Place a notch in the lower portion of the pocket closest to the center front.

3. Measure and mark corresponding points on the pants front and back waist and side.

4. If constructing the pocket from lining or fabric other than fashion fabric, cut a facing piece from fashion fabric to reduce pocket bulk. This will give the appearance at the pocket opening that the whole pocket has been cut from your fashion fabric. The facing is made from the pocket piece by tracing the side edge of the pocket and extending the tracing a minimum of 2 in. in toward the body of the pocket at the top and bottom. Draw a straight or slightly curved line (a French curve is helpful here), connecting the top and bottom edges. Finish this edge with an appropriate seam finish if needed. This facing edge can be directly topstitched to the pocket. Baste the remaining facing-piece edges to the pocket piece at the side.

Side-opening pocket

To eliminate the need for a zipper in your pants, you can modify the inseam pocket instructions to create an opening on the left side through the pocket in the following way.

1. Increase the width of the pocket 2 in. at the waist edge. The mark on the horizontal waist seam should be 5 in. from the side. Increase the depth 2 in. to 13 in. at the deepest part of the pocket. On the long pocket edge opposite the side seam, measure down 8 in. from the upper edge, and mark a point ⅝ in. in from the edge. Clip to that point. Form a narrow hem on each pocket piece (fold under ¼ in. then ⅜ in. and machine-stitch) along this edge. This finished edge will remain open and take the place of a zipper opening.

2. Complete construction of the side-opening pocket as instructed on your pattern guide sheet for inseam pockets, but leave the long hemmed edge open.

3. Stitch the pocket pieces together from the lower dot on the side seam to the clip. Seam-finish the pocket between the dot and side seam as needed.

4. Match the side seams and lower edge of the pocket pieces. Stitch the seam between the lower dot and the hem.

5. Modify the waistband length. Waistband length will be waist size as fitted, plus two seam allowances and the width of one pocket at the waist edge plus 1¼ in. for the closure extension.

Zippers

When selecting a zipper, it is important to choose the proper length as well as the proper type for the application you intend to use. Although pattern notions often list a 7-in.-long zipper as a requirement, I prefer an opening that's a little longer so I don't have to squeeze into my pants and put stress on the zipper. Therefore I select a 9-in. zipper, set it slightly below the zipper-stop mark, and then shorten it at the top if I am installing a waistband. You can choose from three appropriate types of zippers for pants: conventional, invisible, and special purpose.

General guidelines for zippers

- Reinforce the wrong side of the seam allowances where the zipper will be installed with ¾-in.-wide strips of fusible interfacing slightly longer than the zipper opening.
- Purchase a zipper longer than the pattern calls for.
- Finish seam allowances before starting the zipper.

SHORTENING A ZIPPER

Zippers can easily be shortened. If the edge will be finished with a waistband, shorten the zipper from the top. If the edge will be finished with a facing, shorten the zipper from the bottom.

From the top

1. Install the zipper, placing the bottom stop at the desired length.

2. Open the zipper.

3. Stitch a bar tack by hand or machine-stitch over the teeth on one side of the zipper in the seam allowance.

4. Cut off the excess zipper even with the raw edge of the garment.

From the bottom

1. Close the zipper and measure the desired length. Add 1 in. for an invisible zipper.

2. Zigzag across the coil or teeth 8 to 10 times.

3. Cut the zipper $\frac{1}{2}$ in. below the stitching.

4. Install the zipper.

- Press seam allowances open except for the invisible zipper application.
- Whenever possible, apply the zipper while the garment is flat. If fit is questionable or the garment includes special design features, apply the zipper later or when instructed on your pattern guide sheet.
- Preshrink the zipper unless it is 100% polyester.
- Press the fold out of the zipper tape from the wrong side.
- If you purchased a longer zipper, a portion of the unstitched zipper will hang off the garment above the waist. Follow the instructions for shortening a zipper (see the sidebar above).

Pinless centered zipper (basted seam method)

This is one of the most used conventional applications. It is easy and appears uniform on the outside of the garment. It is most often used in center front and center back seams. It can emphasize a design feature and is suitable for medium- to heavy-weight fabrics. You'll find $\frac{1}{4}$-in. wash-away double-sided basting tape and $\frac{1}{2}$-in. transparent tape helpful in the construction process. If applying a waistline facing rather than a waistband, use the facing application technique after installing the zipper.

Installing the zipper

1. Baste the seamline closed from the waist edge to the zipper stop mark. The seam at the waist edge must be exactly even, or one side of the zipper and waistband will be higher than the other.

2. With the zipper faceup, place the sticky side of $\frac{1}{4}$-in. double-sided basting tape on the top side of the zipper. The basting tape should be even with each long edge of the zipper tape. Finger press firmly in place. Peel off the paper layer of the basting tape.

3. Place the zipper facedown on the seam allowance with the bottom stop of the zipper slightly above or below the zipper stop marking. Roll and finger press the zipper down, making sure the zipper teeth are centered exactly on the seamline.

4. Attach the zipper foot to your machine. Position the needle to the side of the zipper being sewn (with the needle closest to the teeth and the foot farthest away).

5. On the right side, center ½-in. transparent tape over the seam, ending the tape at the pattern zipper stop mark.

6. On the right side, begin stitching at the bottom of the tape on the center seam then up each side. Follow the edge of the tape to keep your stitching straight. Move the needle position or the zipper foot to stitch the second side.

7. Remove the ½-in. transparent tape. Press the zipper from the wrong side along the stitching lines but not over the zipper teeth.

8. From the right side, carefully remove the seam basting.

Facing a centered zipper after installation
1. Pin the facing to the garment edge, right sides together. Turn both ends of the facing back ⅝ in.; trim to ½ in. (see the photo above, background).

2. Stitch the facing to the pants. Grade, clip, and understitch the facing seam allowances.

3. Turn and press the facing to the inside and slipstitch to the zipper tape (see the photo above, foreground).

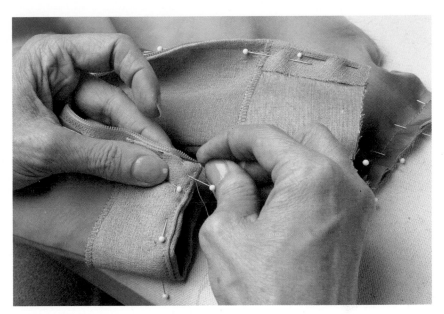

To finish a facing along a conventional zipper opening, fold back the facing seam allowances and pin. Sew the facing to the waist edge. Slipstitch in place, making sure the facing clears the zipper.

Fly zipper (basted seam method)

In this application, the front of the zipper laps from the right to the left for women's pants. A fly shield is not necessary on women's pants. If you are installing a fly zipper for the first time, I do not recommend including a fly shield—it makes an easy procedure more difficult.

Procedure
1. Interface the wrong side of the fly extensions with fusible interfacing (see the top photo on p. 108).

Apply fusible interfacing to reinforce the fabric and provide smooth pucker-free topstitching.

With the fronts basted, stitched, and pressed open, measure and mark ½ in. from the center on the left fly extension.

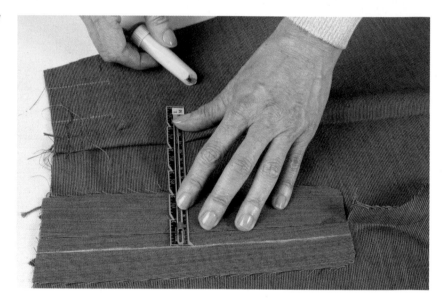

2. Finish the front crotch seam edges and fly extensions if needed.

3. Stitch the two pants fronts together on the crotch seam, beginning 1½ in. from the inside leg seam up to a point ¼ in. below the zipper stop mark. Baste the remaining fronts closed on the center front line to the waist edge. Clip the seam allowance to the stitching below the facing extensions so they can be pressed open and flat.

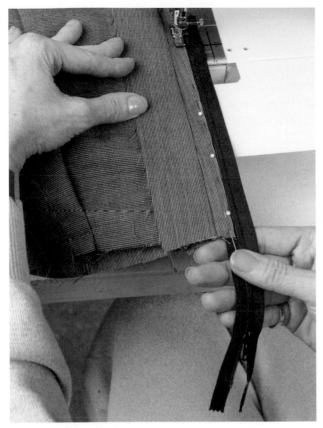

Stitch using a zipper foot, with the pressed edge aligned with the zipper coil.

Stitch the second side of the zipper to the fly extension only.

4. Working from the wrong side, mark a line on the left fly extension ½ in. from and parallel to the center front (see the bottom photo on the facing page). Press only the extension under on this line.

5. With the closed zipper faceup, pin the folded extension close to the coil. The zipper stop should be even with the stop mark.

6. With the needle to the right of the zipper foot, stitch through the extension and zipper tape only, close to the fold edge, from bottom to top (see the left photo above).

7. Open out the pants with the wrong side up, and smooth and flatten the zipper.

8. With the zipper facedown, pin the unstitched side of the zipper tape to the unstitched fly extension *only*. Stitch through the middle of the tape and the fly extension only (see the right photo above).

9. Turn the garment right side up and smooth the fabric flat. Mark the zipper topstitching line on the right front (as the garment is worn) beginning at a point ¼ in. below the zipper-stop mark. Removable tape, a disappearing marking pen, tailor's chalk, or basting work well for this step. The width of the topstitching line from the center front can vary. I prefer 1 in. to 1¼ in. Place pins through all thicknesses to ensure the fabric stays flat, or make a fly-zipper template and tape to the pants as a guide (see the left photo below).

10. With the needle positioned to the left of the foot, topstitch from the bottom to the top on the marked guideline.

11. Horizontally bartack at the bottom of the topstitching and seam intersection for about ¼ in.

12. Open the basting along the center front.

For even topstitching on the fly, you can make your own template from the pants pattern. Use a material that is transparent so you can trace the pattern and rigid enough to hold its shape.

The finished fly zipper should be even and flat and should not buckle.

Invisible zipper (open-seam method)

This zipper is hidden in the seam—only the pull tab shows (see the photo at right). This application does not detract from the fabric or pants style. It is suitable for any weight fabric and any seam where you would put another type zipper. To install this zipper, you'll need a universal invisible zipper foot (a special adapter may be necessary for your machine).

Procedure

1. Open the zipper. With the iron on the synthetic setting, press the coils flat from the wrong side so the two rows of stitching show (see the bottom photo at right).

2. Pin the right sides of the zipper and fabric together, with the coil on the seam-line and the top stop of the zipper ¼ in. to ⅜ in. below the seamline.

3. Line up the center marking of the invisible zipper foot with the machine needle, or as instructed by the directions that come with the foot. With the right groove of the foot over the coil, stitch the zipper until the foot hits the slider (see the left photo on p. 112). Backstitch.

4. Pin the right side of the free zipper tape to the right side of the remaining pants side. Be sure the zipper is not twisted at the bottom. Place the coil on the

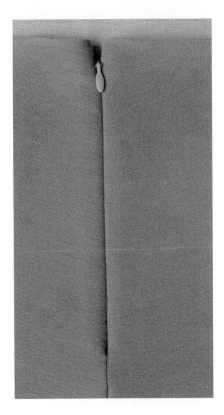

A correctly sewn invisible zipper is just that!

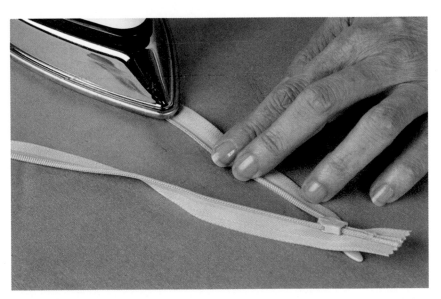

When ironing an invisible zipper, you will be able to noticeably uncurl the zipper coil.

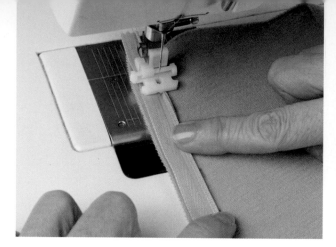

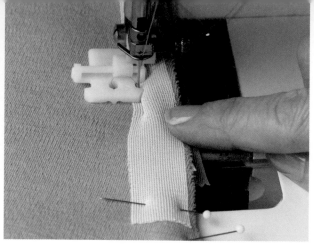

To sew the first half of the invisible zipper, use the right-hand notch of the invisible zipper foot.

Without catching the zipper, sew the pants sections together, beginning slightly above and to the left of the last zipper stitching. Note that the zipper opening has been reinforced with fusible interfacing.

seamline and the top stop the exact distance below the previously stitched side.

5. Be sure the center marking of the foot is still lined up with the machine needle. With the left groove of the foot over the coil, stitch the zipper until the foot hits the slider. Backstitch.

6. Close the zipper. Slide the foot to the left side so the needle is in the outer notch. Pin the pants sections right sides together along the seam. Pull the end of the zipper out of the way and lower the needle by hand slightly above and to the left of the last stitching. Lower the foot and stitch the seam for at least 2 in. (see the right photo above). Complete the remaining seam with your machine's regular foot.

7. Using a zipper foot, stitch each side of the bottom zipper tape to each seam allowance.

Facing an invisible zipper after installation

1. On the facing at the zipper-opening edge, trim off the ⅝-in. seam allowance on both sides.

2. Pin the facing and garment right sides together, matching edges at the zipper only.

3. Using your machine's zipper foot, stitch ⅜ in. from the edge, parallel to the zipper opening through the facing, zipper tape, and garment.

4. Realign the facing, matching seams and waist edge (see the top photo on the facing page). A fold will form at the zipper.

5. Pin then stitch the facing to the pants along the waist edge (see the center photo on the facing page). Grade, clip, and understitch the seam allowance (see the bottom photo on the facing page). Press.

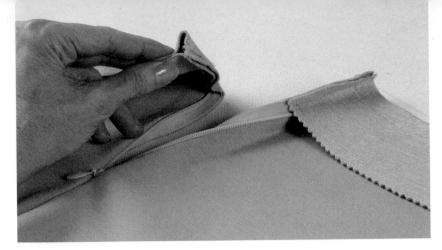

Realign the trimmed edge of the facing with the zipper edge and stitch. Since the garment is now longer than the facing, a fold will form.

Stitch the fold down when stitching the facing to the pants.

Grade, clip, and understitch. The result is a neat, clean finish to your invisible zipper facing.

Finishing the Crotch Seam

Turn one leg of your pants inside out and the other leg right side out. Slip one leg into the other, making sure right sides are together. Match and pin at the inside leg seam, center front, and center back. Include a piece of stay tape when pinning and stitching the deepest part of the crotch curve (see the photo below). Double-stitch and trim the seam (see Seams and Finishes on p. 100) through the deepest part of the crotch curve. Finish the seam allowances above the curve.

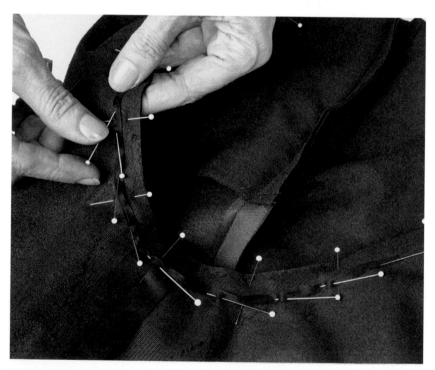

These synthetic suede pants have a crotch reinforced in two ways: The angles of the pants legs have been reinforced at the crotch point with fusible interfacing, and stay tape is sewn in along the seamline.

Attaching the Lining

Lining should be sewn in the same way as the fashion fabric but without the zipper. For the zipper opening, the methods that follow will give you a very neat, clean, professional-looking zipper opening that will be simple to secure to the zipper tape with hand stitching.

Lining preparation for a fly zipper

When installing a lining in pants with a fly zipper, the zipper is actually off-center while the opening is on center front. Because the lining is retrofitted around the zipper, the finishing at the bottom stop can look less than professional.

These steps will lead you through the process to get a geometrical zipper opening in the lining that is neat, flat, and pucker free from bottom to top. Do not stitch the lining center front crotch seam until after all marking, folding, and trimming is complete.

1. On both pieces of the lining mark the center front, bottom zipper stop, and a point ½ in. below the zipper stop.

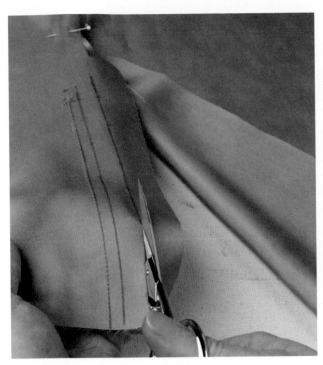 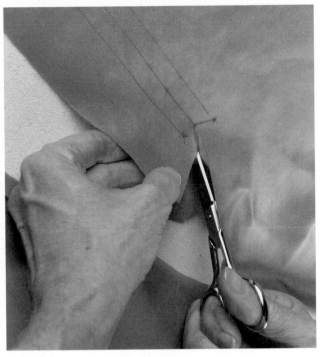

When all measurements are marked, cut away the left fly extension ½ in. from the foldline.

Clip the right extension from the edge straight across to the mark ½ in. below the zipper stop, diagonally to the center, then diagonally to the bottom of the foldline.

2. On the right side of the fabric and left-hand side of the lining as it will be positioned in the pants, draw a line parallel to and ¼ in. from the center front toward the fly extension. Label this "foldline."

3. Trim away the excess fly extension ½ in. from the foldline (see the left photo above).

4. Fold the left side of the lining to the wrong side on the foldline.

5. For the foldline on the right-hand side of the lining, mark two lines parallel to the center front, ½ in. and 1 in. from the center front toward the *body* of the pants. Extend the 1-in. line so it is ½ in. below the zipper stop mark.

6. Beginning at the edge of the fly extension and ½ in. below the zipper stop mark, cut horizontally to the center front, then diagonally up to the midpoint mark and down to the bottom of the foldline, forming a triangle (see the right photo above).

7. Beginning at the waist edge, cut on the middle line to the top of the zipper stop (at the point of the triangle), cutting off the excess fly extension.

Press the triangle and the long edge to the wrong side along the foldlines.

With the wrong sides together, stitch the crotch seam with a ⅝-in. seam allowance. Stitch a second time using a ⅜-in. seam allowance.

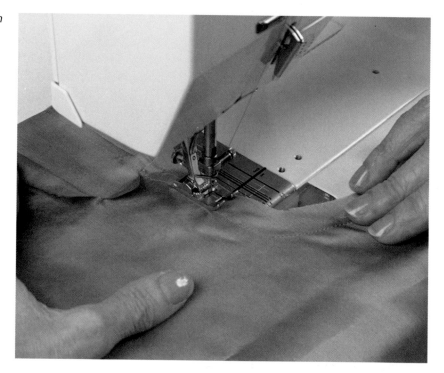

8. Fold the remaining fabric to the wrong side on the foldline and press.

9. To square off the bottom, fold the triangle formed by the previous trimming to the wrong side and press (see the top photo on the facing page).

10. Sew the lining crotch seam with a ⅝-in. seam allowance, stopping the center front crotch seam at a point ½ in. below the zipper stop. Stitch the seam again with a ⅜-in. seam allowance (see the bottom photo on the facing page). Trim close to the ⅜-in. seamline. Press the crotch seam toward the right front.

11. Arrange the lining around the zipper slightly back from the coil on either side to avoid catching. Pin (see the top photo at right). Slipstitch in place. Remove the pins and press lightly, being careful not to press over the zipper teeth.

Lining preparation for other zippers For other zipper installations, prepare the lining opening as follows:

1. At the zipper stop opening, cut into the seam allowance up to the stitching (see the bottom photo at right). Then cut down at a 45° angle ¼ in. to ⅜ in., forming a triangle.

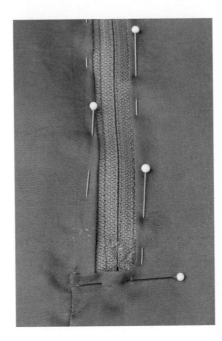

The finished lining will work perfectly with the off-center placement of a fly zipper.

Prepare the lining for a conventional or invisible zipper opening by sewing the lining together up to the zipper stop opening. Clip the seam allowance, then cut down diagonally ¼ in. to ⅜ in. Mark before you cut.

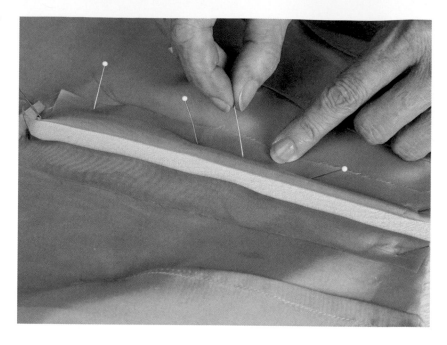

With the seam allowance open and the edges turned to the wrong side, pin then press in place.

2. Turn the seam allowances and small triangle formed to the wrong side. Pin (see the photo above), then press in place. Note: The turned-back seam allowances will be greater than ⅝ in. to allow room around the zipper teeth so the lining won't get caught.

After the zipper opening in the lining has been prepared according to the type of zipper installed, turn the lining inside out. Slip the lining into the pants so wrong sides are together. Match darts, seams, and zipper openings. Pin. Baste the lining to the pants waist edge using a ½-in. seam allowance. Slipstitch the lining to the zipper tape.

Waistband

The waist finish is an important part of the comfort and appearance of your pants. Finishes will vary with the pattern and current styles, but design principles and basic construction will remain the same. If you are a beginning sewer, it is best to follow your pattern guide sheet. Those more experienced can try some of the variations discussed in Chapter 6 (see p. 143).

Waistband comfort is dependent on proper fit and type of interfacing used. If you have trouble with your waistband curling during wear, consider making the waistband slightly larger or narrower or using a firmer type of interfacing. Fusible

118

Ease the waistband by using a large stitch size, then pulling up stitches every few inches with a pin.

interfacings tend to be softer and more comfortable than the sew-in types like Ban-Rol or Armoflexxx. However, the softer interfacings do not hold their shape as well. Professional-looking waistbands should always be an even width, flat and smooth with no bulges, and cut with one long edge along the selvage edge. By cutting the waistband on the selvage, the facing or inside edge of the band is already finished. Unnecessary bulk is eliminated because the seam allowance doesn't need to be turned to the inside of the band. If not cut on the lengthwise grain, the band must be interfaced to prevent stretching.

The following guidelines will aid you in the ease of application of your waist finish and keep it the exact size as when applied throughout the life of your garment.

Guidelines

The pants waist needs to be slightly larger (by about ¾ in.) than the band. Ease-stitch the pants to fit the waistband. This will pucker the fabric slightly but won't cause gathers. This technique will reduce the size of the pants to fit. With a pin, gently pull up stitches every few inches, taking care not to break the stitching (see the photo above). Evenly distribute ease across the front between the side seams. The amount and placement may vary depending on your figure. If more or less ease is needed, alter at the side seams, pleats, or darts.

I pin-fit the waistband to the garment before attaching it. That way I can determine how much the pants need to be eased to precisely fit the waistband. To ease-stitch the pants, I use a ½-in. seam allowance and a #3 to #4 stitch length (10 stitches per inch), depending on the fabic thickness.

If you're applying a waist facing or if you're not using a stable fusible interfacing, stay the waistline with tape following the directions for staying the crotch seam on p. 114.

Procedure

The following instructions are for a fitted straight waistband, the most common type of waistband. The waistband will lie flat and provide a clean finish on the inside. The waistband size is usually predetermined by your pattern. However, you can make changes for fitting or style reasons. For the length, use your body measurement or the determined length from fitting, then add two ⅝-in. seam allowances (1¼ in. total) plus a minimum 1¼ in. for the extension (room for a fastener).

A different amount may be needed for a fly zipper depending on how far the zipper is off-set from the center front when installed (this will be a concern only if you modified your pattern for a fly zipper). Make sure the length of your waistband finishes the entire waist edge. Then add two seam allowances and an extension allowance. Add an additional 3 in. to 5 in. for an inseam pocket opening or the width of the pocket at the waist edge. The cut width of the waistband will equal two times the desired finished width plus two ⅝-in. seam allowances.

Preparing the waistband

1. Finish one long edge of the waistband if it's not cut on the selvage.

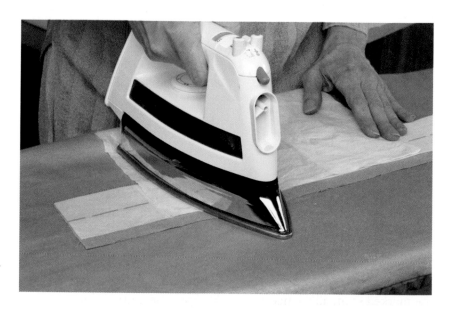

Fuse the precut interfacing to the waistband using a dampened paper towel over the interfacing.

2. Cut the interfacing the length of the waistband (eliminate seam allowances on interfacing if using fusible with Ban-Rol, Armoflexxx, or hair canvas).

3. Precisely mark ⅝ in. along the long unfinished edge.

4. Fuse interfacing to the wrong side of the waistband, aligning the edge with the ⅝-in. seamline. If the interfacing halves are uneven widths, align the narrower side with the marking. Press for 10 to 15 seconds along the seamline, overlapping spots slightly as you move the iron. Place a dampened paper towel over the interfacing when fusing (see the photo on the facing page). If you incorrectly position the interfacing with the glue side up, there's no messy iron to clean. It also adds a bit more moisture.

5. Mark off the seam allowances and the extension amount.

Applying the waistband

1. Check the fit of the waistband to the pants by pin fitting it first. Adjust the ease on the pants as previously described.

2. If attaching belt loops, position them at this time.

3. With right sides together, pin the long unfinished edge of the waistband to the pants. Match the marked seam allowance and

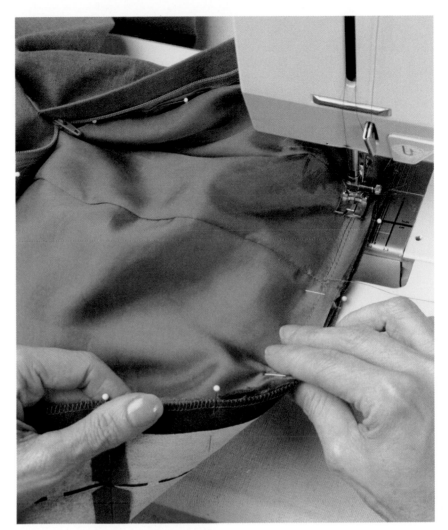

When attaching the waistband to the garment, have the garment on top so you can control the ease and avoid puckers on the garment side.

lines on the waistband to the pants opening edges.

4. With the waistband on the bottom and the garment on top, stitch the waistband to the garment from the zipper opening edge to edge (see the photo above).

5. Fold the ends of the waistband in half (perforation

Cut the corners of the waistband
before turning to eliminate bulk.

Press the seam toward the
waistband, using the end of your
ironing board or a tailor's ham to
retain the curve of the waistband.

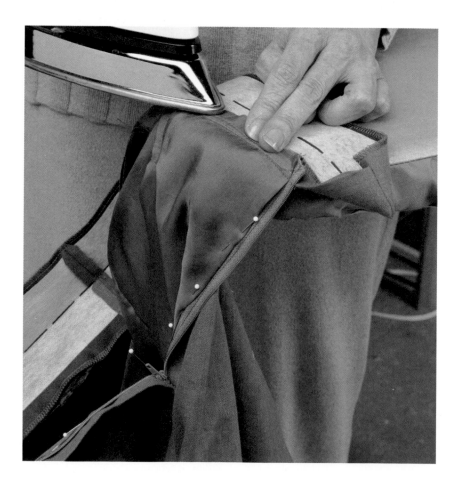

makes this foolproof) with right sides together and stitch each end along the seamline. Trim the seams to ¼ in., then cut the corners diagonally (see the top photo on the facing page). Press.

6. Press the waist seam toward the waistband. Then turn the waistband right side out. Pin the waistband in place, making sure it is an even width. Turn seam allowances to the inside of the waistband on the extension end, matching edges. Pin to hold in place. Complete the waistband attachment by edgestitching from end to end on the right side, ⅛ in. from the waist seam on the waistband. The long, inside, finished edge of the waistband will be caught in this stitching and permanently secured.

7. Press over the end of the ironing board or a tailor's ham (see the bottom photo on the facing page).

Closures

Special-purpose waistband hook-and-bar sets are sturdy and well suited for the strain a waistband will get. The number and kind will depend on the length of your extension. The waistband should be secured at the opening edge as well as at the extension end of the waistband. If you prefer a button and buttonhole on a classic band, try my method. Make a buttonhole, but don't cut it open. Sew the button on top of the buttonhole, and then apply the hook-and-bar closures on the underside. It looks like the real thing, and the closure stays precisely put.

To attach a hook-and-bar set, first attach the hook to the wrong side of the overlap portion of the waistband, ¼ in. from the finished open end and centered on the waistband. Attach the hook and bar using a buttonhole stitch. Begin with a single strand of thread and knot the end. At the hook position on the placement side, take a small stitch. Take a second stitch in the same place. When you stitch the hook portion, use a buttonhole stitch and only stitch through the waistband facing. *Do not* stitch through to the right side.

To position the straight bar portion, attach it to the hook with the zipper closed. Lap the overlap portion of the waistband onto the underlap extension portion, positioning the waistband edges evenly as they will be when worn. Make sure the waistband fit is smooth and straight above the zipper.

Find where the straight bar portion lines up on the underlap of the waistband both vertically

Stitching Hooks and Bars Using a Buttonhole Stitch

1. Take two stitches on the wrong side of the overlap ¼ in. from the end.

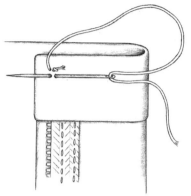

2. Bring the needle up through the hole of the hook and work a buttonhole stitch, keeping the thread loop under both the point and the eye of the needle.

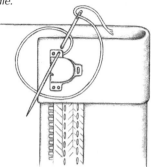

3. Continue working from right to left until all holes are filled with thread and three sides are secured.

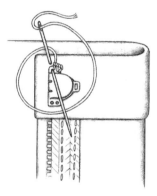

4. Mark the position of the bar on the underlap extension with pins.

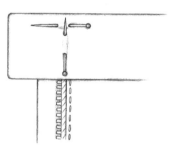

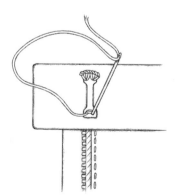

5. Begin stitching as in step 1. Work using a buttonhole stitch (as shown on top of bar) or in and out as illustrated on the bottom.

and horizontally, and mark this location with two pins. This is the sewing position for the straight bar. Now unhook the eye portion from the hook and position it according to your pin markings. Because there are two holes at each end, you can either stitch around the eyes using the buttonhole stitch as before, or as a time-saving technique, you can stitch in and out of each pair of holes. Because this stitching will not show, you can stitch completely through both layers of fabric. You may also stitch the eye portion by machine as a timesaver.

Hems

Whether or not you like your pants to break at the front hemline is a personal preference. The more tapered or tighter the leg is, the shorter the pants can be. Lengthen the hem at the center back leg by ½ in. if necessary to cover the heel of your shoe. Lengthening it more can require a facing. Because the hemline becomes more angled or shaped, it is difficult to turn up a straight 1½-in. hem and have it be flat and smooth. A narrow machine hem, however, is possible. I adjust hem length per pair of pants, that is, according to style, fabric, and shoes of the moment. Besides, it will all change next season. Make notes of what you like and looks best

on you as you make various styles of pants. For cuffs, see p. 153.

A well-finished hem should be inconspicuous on the right side; uniform in width; flat, smooth, not bulky; appropriate in width for your pants' style and fabric; and stitched evenly and securely.

Procedure

1. After determining the length, press the hem from the wrong side. For classic pants with a straight hem, trim the hem allowance to 1½ in.

2. Trim seams in the hem allowance to ¼ in. to reduce bulk. Clip each seam allowance to the stitching at the hemline.

3. At the side seams and inseams, lengthen the hem by ⅛ in. Even though you're making these areas slightly longer, they will appear the same length due to the slight bulkiness when the hem is finished.

4. Apply an edge finish to the right side of the hem allowance. The edge can be stitched and pinked, serged, bound, or edged with seam tape.

5. Hand- or machine-stitch in place. If hand hemming, flat stitch or blindstitch the hem edge.

Setting Creaselines

Pants with darts
The creaseline in darted pants begins 3 in. above the crotch level and extend through the middle of the leg to the hem.

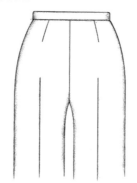

Pants with pleats
For pants with pleats, the creaseline will extend from the main front pleat through the center of the leg to the hem.

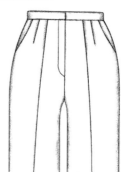

Front crease for darted trousers
To set the creaseline, fold back the upper leg, matching the inseam to the side seam. Use a steam iron and clapper.

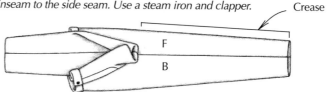

Front crease for pleated trousers

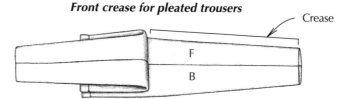

Back crease
Set the creaseline in back as for the front. The creaseline will end at crotch level for both styles.

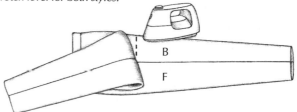

Making a French Tack

Stitched and pinked edge

WS lining

WS pants

French tack

1. *Bring a single knotted thread up from the wrong side of the pants hem.*

2. *Take three or four stitches between the garment and the lining hem. Stitches should go in and come out at the same point. Each thread stitch should be about 1¼ in. long between the garment and lining.*

3. *Work a buttonhole stitch over these threads, keeping the stitches close together.*

6. When the lining hem is finished, it should be ¾ in. to 1 in. shorter than the finished pants length. Finish the raw edge of the hem allowance. Turn the hem to the wrong side and machine topstitch in place.

7. Pull the lining legs up through the pants toward the waist. Do a final touch-up pressing on the fashion fabric. Set the creaselines if desired (see the drawing on the facing page).

8. Press the hem on the fashion fabric. To prevent a ridge line from showing through to the right side of the fabric, first butt a piece of scrap fabric against the hem edge where it attaches to the garment.

9. Attach the lining to the hem allowance with a 1½-in. French tack at the side seams and inseams (see the drawing above).

6 | *Stylizing Your Pattern*

A successful design begins with a well-fitting pattern so that no fitting problems are passed on. Because design changes can alter the original fit of your pants to varying degrees, you should be familiar with how your customized pants fit and feel. Study your pattern and note where you have made adjustments, what it looks like, and how it differs from the unaltered commercial pattern you began with.

Before you make any changes to your pattern, always trace a copy onto which you will make your changes, preserving your original for further work and reference. You can enhance or completely change the look of your original pants by executing some of the variations on the following pages. Simple style changes, the addition of design details, and an array of fabrics make for limitless combinations. You may decide to try only one depending on your level of confidence and skill or to combine several into one new pattern.

Analyze your new design carefully and don't get stuck in a fabric rut. It may call for a completely different fabric, maybe one you've never worked with. You're limited only by your imagination and creativity. Have fun! That's what it's all about. If you're unsure, choose an inexpensive fabric on which to experiment or use some of the outdated fabric in your stash. Fabric is a small investment compared to the wealth of knowledge you gain and the pleasure and satisfaction you get from a self-created project.

Transforming Darts

A basic pants pattern with darts opens up endless design possibilities. Darts shape and fit, but they are not especially beautiful and can be boring after the second pair of pants; however, they can be easily transformed into tuck darts, gathers, pleats, or flare. These options maintain the fitting control of the original dart(s) but look different. The difference between them is how they are marked and sewn.

Tuck darts

Tuck darts are partially stitched darts. To make tuck darts,

measure the length of the dart(s) to be converted from wide end to point. Divide this distance in half and mark. This mark is where you will stop stitching. Sew as you would a traditional dart, beginning at the widest end and stopping at the midpoint marked (see the drawing below).

Gathers

Dart-equivalent gathers at the waist are comfortable, not full, give a softer look, and work well for those of us with full tummies or fleshy padding between the waist and hip. The dart(s) can be completely eliminated, but the dart take-up (interior distance between the dart legs) must be accounted for by gathering. The waistline fit will remain the

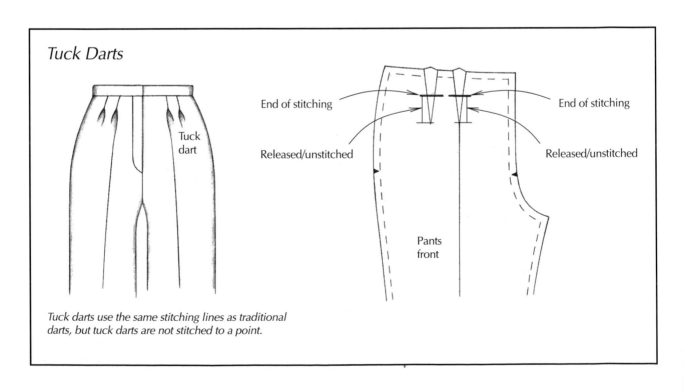

Tuck Darts

Tuck dart

End of stitching

Released/unstitched

End of stitching

Released/unstitched

Pants front

Tuck darts use the same stitching lines as traditional darts, but tuck darts are not stitched to a point.

same. To convert one dart to gathers, place a dot at the wide end of each dart leg (stitching line). The distance between the dots will be drawn up with gathering stitches so the dots meet (see the drawing at right). This gathering is done in the normal construction sequence when it's time to sew the darts. To true the waist edge for gathers, draw a gently outwardly curved line from the side to center front. Repeat for the back if desired.

If there is more than one dart, and the take-up of the darts, as well as the distance between the two darts, is to be gathered (for added fullness), the amount of the additional gathered fullness must be added to the waist, or the waist will be too small. Measure the waist space between the inner legs of the two darts and add this amount to the side waist. To true the pattern, draw a line from the marked waist addition and taper it to "0" at the hip, following the side-seam curve. Repeat for the back if desired.

Pleats

For a traditional trouser look, convert the front dart(s) into pleat(s). This is a winning style for just about all figure types. An easy way to convert waist darts to pleats during construction is to fold one dart leg over to meet the other on the right side of your fabric at the waist edge.

Gathers

Single dart converted to gathers

Both darts and space between them converted to gathers

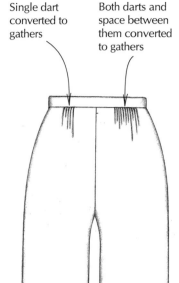

Single dart converted to gathers

The dart area below the waist is not sewn as a dart. The area between dots is gathered so the dots meet.

Gather

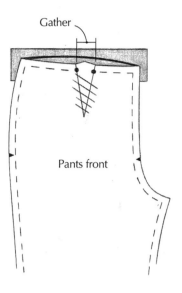

Pants front

Two darts converted to gathers

Gathers

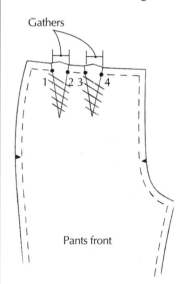

Pants front

The area to be gathered will be equivalent to the distance between the darts (dots 1 and 2, and dots 3 and 4) and the garment area between dots 2 and 3.

Gathers   True waist edge

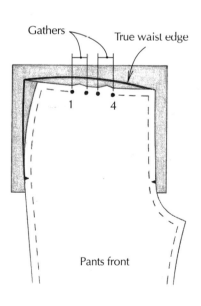

Pants front

Measure the distance between darts and add this amount to the side-waist seam.

Working with the pattern over a large piece of paper, create a waist pleat by cutting and spreading the front from waist to hem. Work by pinning the pattern to the surface until the spread at the waist is twice the amount of the finished pleat size, then tape in place.

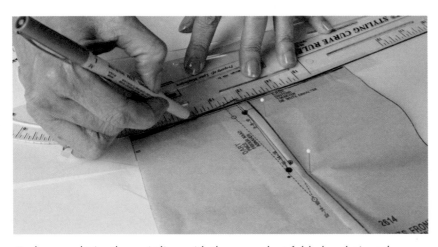

Redraw and trim the waistline with the new pleat folded and pinned.

Baste the pleat at the waist seam to hold in place until the waistband is applied.

1. For fuller, more generous pleats, modify your front pattern. Locate the dart leg closest to center front. Draw a line parallel to the grainline from the intersection of the waist and dart leg to the bottom of your pattern. Place see-through paper underneath this line.

2. Cut from the waist to but not through the hem. Spread the pattern at the waist twice the distance of the desired finished-pleat size. For example, a 2-in. spread will give you a 1-in. finished pleat. If your pattern has only one front dart, incorporate the dart into the pleat by subtracting the dart take-up from the amount of spread. Using the above example, you would spread the pattern 1½ in. if the dart take-up is ½ in. (see the top photo at left).

3. The width of the second pleat is the sum of the two dart take-ups. For example, if the take-up of each dart is ½ in. and there are two darts, then the width of the second pleat will be 1 in. To mark the second pleat, begin at the dart leg closest to the side. Measure 1 in. along the waist toward center front and mark.

4. Fold and pin each pleat in the desired direction (toward the center front, toward the side, or with each pleat edge to the center of the pleat). With the pleat(s) pinned closed, redraw the waist edge between the side and center front with a gently curved line, as shown in the bottom photo at left. Trim the pattern on the drawn line for the new cutting line. Unpin the pleat(s).

Adding fullness by spreading your pattern, as described here, creates more generous pleat(s) and a bit more fullness in the leg yet gives you the same fit in the waist.

Hint: Before attaching the waistband, fold pleats on one side of the front in one direction and in the opposite direction on the other side. See which is more becoming. Once you've decided, fold both the same way and sew on the waistband.

Flare

One method of creating leg flare is to move the dart(s) to the hem. Dart(s) can be transformed into hemline flare without affecting the fit. A portion or all of each dart(s) can be moved to the bottom of the leg, with the width of the pants leg below the crotch gradually increased. Since the degree of fullness can be controlled when adding this dart equivalent flare, most figure types will benefit from this easy style change.

1. Draw a line parallel to the grainline from dart point to hem.

2. Cut from the waist to the dart point on one of the dart legs. Cut up from the hem to the dart point but not through it. Keep the pattern flat but do not separate the pattern pieces. Place see-through paper under the pattern. Move one dart leg to the center of the same dart. Tape in

A transformed waist dart adds considerable flare at the hemline.

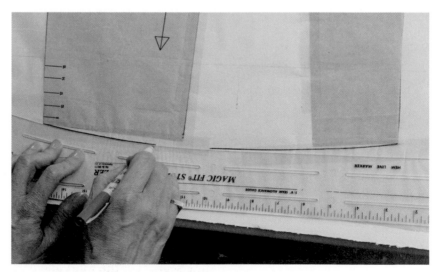

You will have to true the hemline of flared pants, adding a gentle curve.

When narrowing or tapering the pants leg, make sure the finished garment measurement at the hemline is equal to or larger than the circumference measurement over your heel and instep. Otherwise, you won't be able to get your pants over your foot.

place. The hemline area will spread open, as shown in the top photo on p. 133. Because only half of the dart was closed and moved to the hem as flare, the remaining half of the dart at the waist will be sewn as a dart. The fit through the waist will be the same as before half the dart was converted to leg flare.

3. Redraw the hem edge, incorporating a slight curve, as shown in the bottom photo on p. 133. Repeat for the pants back.

4. If more fullness at the lower edge of the pants is desired, transfer the entire width of one or both darts to the hem as flare.

Changing Leg Width

Whether increasing or decreasing leg width, you'll need to consider style and fit. Pictures or pants you already own can guide your style choice and help you decide how much and where to add or subtract the leg width from your present pattern (see the drawing below). The amount and point where the leg width is increased or decreased can affect the style only or fit and style of your pants. If the increase or decrease in leg width is made below the crotchline, the style is changed but the fit remains unaffected as in tapered, flared,

---

Styles of Pants

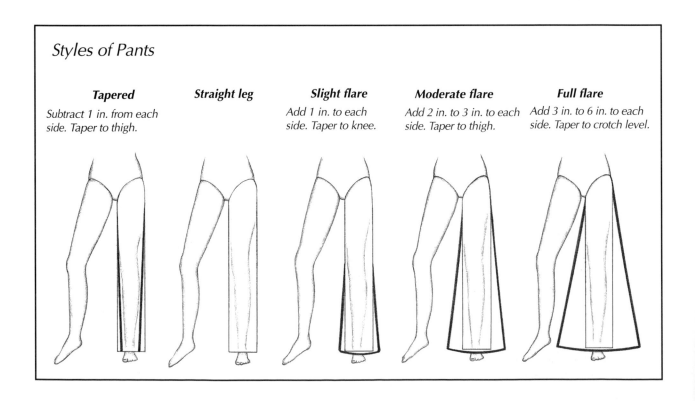

Tapered
Subtract 1 in. from each side. Taper to thigh.

Straight leg

Slight flare
Add 1 in. to each side. Taper to knee.

Moderate flare
Add 2 in. to 3 in. to each side. Taper to thigh.

Full flare
Add 3 in. to 6 in. to each side. Taper to crotch level.

or bell-bottom pants. If a change is made above the crotchline, both the fit and style will be affected as in wide-leg baggies (see the drawing below).

Flaring and tapering

While flaring is a gradual widening of the leg width, tapering is a gradual narrowing. Leg width can be increased or decreased by adding or subtracting at the side and inseam of the front and back pattern pieces. Both flaring and tapering can begin at the knee, crotch, or above the crotch. The fit of your original pattern, personal preference, and current fashion should guide your choices. Straight or wide-leg pants are becoming on most figures. Flared pants are better suited for women with short, thin legs. Tapered pants look well on a figure with short legs, but they are not as complementary for those who are proportionally larger below the waist, have a flat buttocks, or have thin legs.

The amount of ease included in your pattern at the hip, thigh, and knee areas will determine how much room you have to play with when tapering. If narrowing the leg, pin the original garment where you're planning on making the change to get an idea of the look and fit. The pattern knee circumference should measure 1 in. to 1½ in. more than your bent knee measurement so the knee area isn't too tight when bending or sitting.

I prefer a leg width of 41% (for basic slacks) of my full-hip measurement (about 16 in.). This percentage gives a slight taper to my pants leg without being too narrow and emphasizing my hips. Use this percentage as a beginning guide point for your leg width.

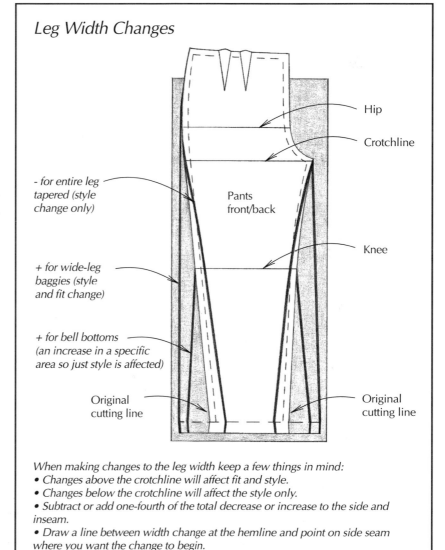

Leg Width Changes

- for entire leg tapered (style change only)

+ for wide-leg baggies (style and fit change)

+ for bell bottoms (an increase in a specific area so just style is affected)

Hip

Crotchline

Pants front/back

Knee

Original cutting line

Original cutting line

When making changes to the leg width keep a few things in mind:
• Changes above the crotchline will affect fit and style.
• Changes below the crotchline will affect the style only.
• Subtract or add one-fourth of the total decrease or increase to the side and inseam.
• Draw a line between width change at the hemline and point on side seam where you want the change to begin.

Changing the leg width means reshaping the hem allowance at the inseam and side leg. Tape see-through paper at the hemline. Fold the paper toward the pants on the hemline and trim on the side edges of the pants. Unfold and trim at the bottom of the hem allowance.

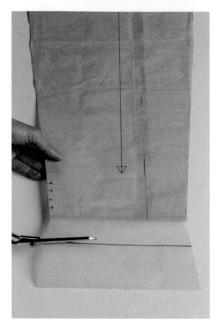

When widening or narrowing your pattern leg width, divide the total amount of increase or decrease by four. Add or subtract one-fourth the total amount of change to the side and inseam front and back pattern at the hemline. If widening, tape a piece of see-through paper 2 in. to 7 in. wide to the side and inseam front leg of the front and back pattern. The width of the added paper should be slightly more than the intended increase. Extend the paper from the lower edge of the hew allowance to the point where you intend the new leg line to blend into your original pattern. If narrowing the leg, mark directly on your pattern.

To complete the new leg line on the side and inseam, draw a line between the newly established width at the hemline and a point farther up the leg. The greater the increase or decrease, the farther up the leg the line can go and the change can begin. If the newly established line extends above the crotchline, the fit will be affected. Below the crotchline only the style will change.

Reshaping the hem allowance

If you've changed the leg width at the hemline, you will need to adjust the shape of the hem allowance on the front and back pattern. If your pattern didn't include a hem allowance, tape tissue to your pattern at the hemline that is wider than your new leg width and that extends below the hemline several inches. On the tissue, draw a line parallel to the hem-line the amount of the hem allowance (1¼ in. to 1½ in.), or the desired width.

To complete the reshaping, fold the hem allowance to the wrong side of the pattern on the hemline. Pin each side to secure. From the right side of the pattern, cut on the side and inseam new leg line from the hemline up to the point where the line blends into your original pattern. Unfold the hem allowance. If you added the hem allowance as previously described, cut away the excess tissue on the drawn line (see the photo above). You now have your new-leg-width pants pattern and correctly shaped hem allowance to fit the new leg line.

Pants Go to Any Length

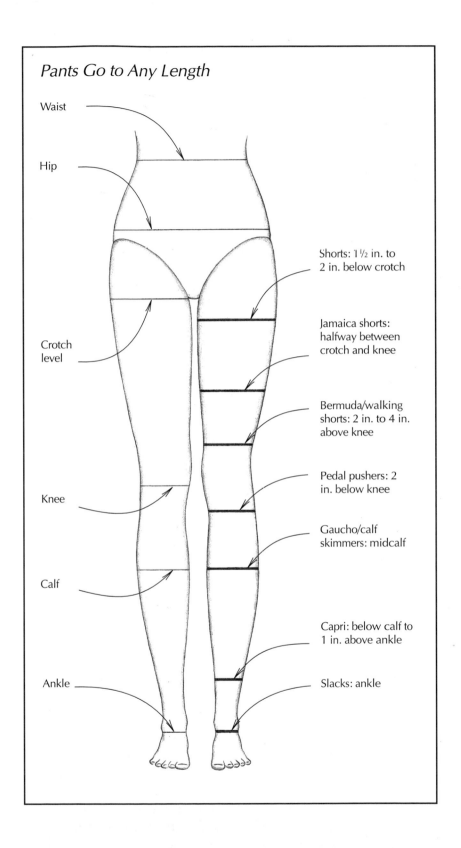

Waist

Hip

Crotch level

Knee

Calf

Ankle

Shorts: 1 1/2 in. to 2 in. below crotch

Jamaica shorts: halfway between crotch and knee

Bermuda/walking shorts: 2 in. to 4 in. above knee

Pedal pushers: 2 in. below knee

Gaucho/calf skimmers: midcalf

Capri: below calf to 1 in. above ankle

Slacks: ankle

Changing Leg Length

Pants length and names vary from season to season. With a few easy changes you can modify the length of your pattern and be currently fashionable, or adapt your pants for a particular occasion or activity (see the drawing on p. 137).

Depending on the style or leg width of your original pattern, you may need to make a slight width increase or decrease at the inside and side leg to suit personal preference or current fashion. Let your wardrobe or RTW garments be your guide. If in doubt before cutting, allow extra seam allowances as a safety margin until after you have checked the fabric fit and look on your body.

Converting your basic pattern

1. Decide on a new length.

For the front and back repeat the following steps.

2. Trace the pattern to its new length.

3. At the new length, measure in ¼ in. to 1 in. at the inseam and side leg edges and mark (¼ in. to ⅜ in. for shorts and Jamaicas, ½ in. for Bermudas and pedal pushers, and 1 in. for longer lengths).

4. Redraw the inseam and side leg edges to crotch level.

5. Add 1 in. to 1½ in. to the finished new length for the hem allowance.

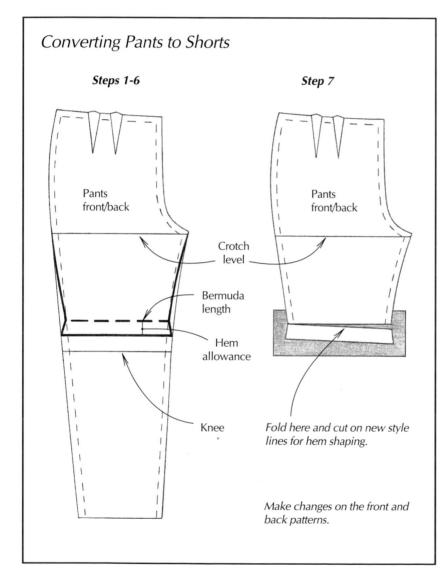

Converting Pants to Shorts

Steps 1-6

Pants front/back

Crotch level

Bermuda length

Hem allowance

Knee

Step 7

Pants front/back

Fold here and cut on new style lines for hem shaping.

Make changes on the front and back patterns.

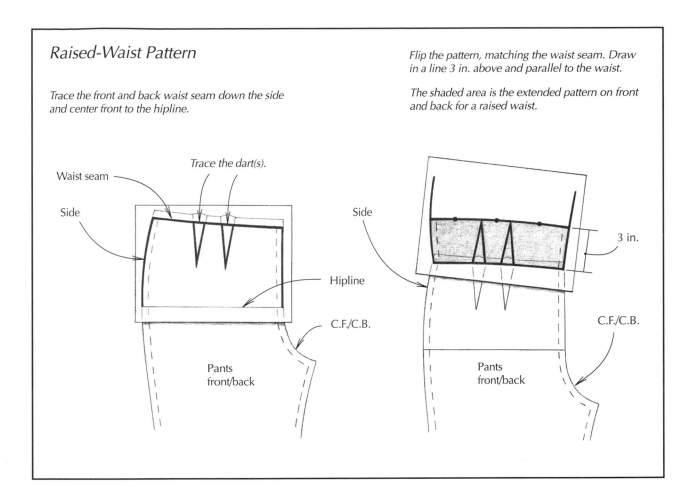

Raised-Waist Pattern

Trace the front and back waist seam down the side and center front to the hipline.

Flip the pattern, matching the waist seam. Draw in a line 3 in. above and parallel to the waist.

The shaded area is the extended pattern on front and back for a raised waist.

Trace the dart(s).

Waist seam

Side

Hipline

C.F./C.B.

Pants front/back

Side

3 in.

C.F./C.B.

Pants front/back

---

6. Fold the pattern to the wrong side along the hemline. Cut along the inseam and side-leg edges for correct hem shaping.

7. For lengths above the knee only (shorts, Jamaicas, and Bermudas), you'll need to make a correction on the inner leg so the pants legs will fit and hang better. At the hemline, slash from the inside leg edge to the side edge. Spread the inside leg edge ⅜ in. to ⅝ in., tapering the spread to "0" at the side edge.

Raised-Waist Pants

This style extends 2½ in. to 3 in. above the natural waist and enhances figures with short legs or a long waist/torso. Since this style has no waistband, once the pattern waist is raised, a facing will need to be made to finish the upper edge. Directions are the same for front and back except for the dart(s) as noted.

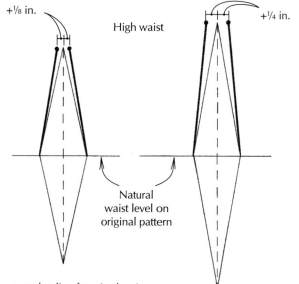

Adjusting Darts for a Raised Waist

Front dart

For front darts, measure ⅛ in. to each side of the point of the raised-waist dart and mark.

Back dart

Draw in a new raised-waist dart line from ¼ in. on each side of the point to the natural waist level.

+⅛ in.

High waist

+¼ in.

Natural waist level on original pattern

Heavy lines = new dart line for raised waist

Regular lines = original dart line as traced on completed pattern

Because wrinkling and curling of a raised waist may occur, interface with a firm interfacing such as hair canvas. Additional support may be added at the seams and darts by using Rigilene, a polyester sew-through flexible boning, available in black and white.

Procedure for the pants

1. Lay see-through paper over the pants from hipline to waist. Trace the waistline seam from side edge to center front. Trace the side edge and center-front edge to the hipline. Trace the darts (see the drawing on p. 139).

2. Remove the paper with the tracings and flip it up so the traced waist seam matches the pattern at the center front and side. Measure 3 in. up from the waist seam into the traced area

and mark with dots. Draw a line through these dots parallel to the waist seam from side to center front to complete the pattern.

3. To correct darts for the raised-waist shaping, redraw them as shown in the drawing at left and following these directions: Extend the centerline of the dart(s) into the raised waist, ending at the dart point. On the front dart(s), increase the dart ⅛ in. on both sides of the original dart at the raised-waist dart point. On the back dart(s), increase the dart ¼ in. on both sides of the original dart at the raised-waist dart point.

Procedure for the facing

1. Trace the completed raised-waist pattern on the front and back from the waist seam up (see the drawing on the facing page).

2. Cut out the dart(s) and butt the remaining pieces together.

3. Retrace the pattern piece, blending a smooth line at the high-waist and waist edge. As an option, the center front can be placed on the fold if the opening is at the side or back to reduce bulk.

4. Repeat for the back. The center back may or may not be cut on the fold, depending on where the garment opening is.

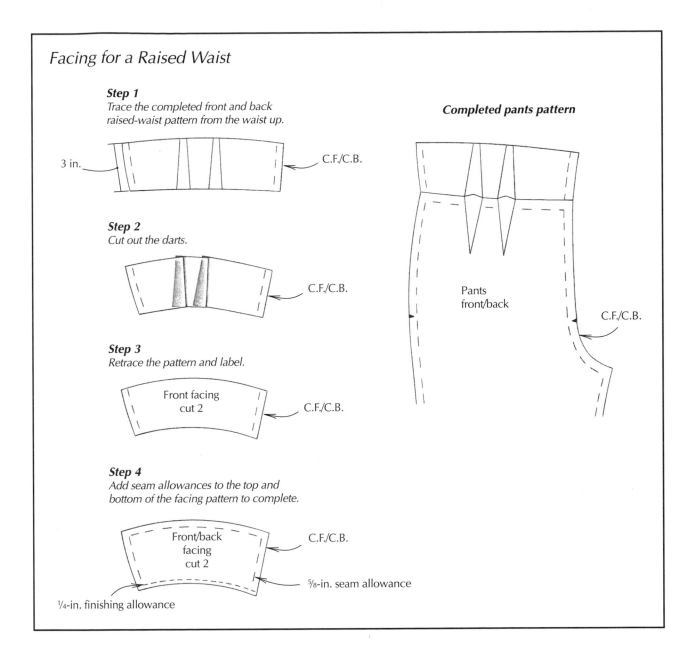

Facing for a Raised Waist

Step 1
Trace the completed front and back
raised-waist pattern from the waist up.

3 in.

C.F./C.B.

Completed pants pattern

Step 2
Cut out the darts.

C.F./C.B.

Step 3
Retrace the pattern and label.

Front facing
cut 2

C.F./C.B.

Pants
front/back

C.F./C.B.

Step 4
Add seam allowances to the top and
bottom of the facing pattern to complete.

Front/back
facing
cut 2

C.F./C.B.

⅝-in. seam allowance

¼-in. finishing allowance

Pull-On Pants

Because these pants are so comfortable, no one should be without them. You probably own some version of this style with a gathered elasticized waist. Fabric choice as well as leg width can influence how you look in this style. Therefore, begin with a leg width that is not excessively tapered in relation to your hip size. If you have a thick waist, large hips, or a protruding tummy, choose a soft, nonbulky fabric that drapes well, such as jersey knit, wool crepe, challis, rayon, or crepe de chine. The following directions are for a self-fabric fold-over casing. Part of the fun of these pants is their ease of construction—no zipper or separate waistband to apply. If you prefer less fullness at the waist, decrease the amount you add at the waist and add a zipper.

Converting your basic pattern

1. Measure your front and back pattern waist with pleats and darts flat (these will not be sewn), minus seam allowances. Since you're measuring half a pattern, add the front and back measurement, then multiply your measurement by two for the total circumference.

2. Tape a large piece of see-through paper under your pattern from the hipline to 6 in. above the waist level. The paper should be several inches wider than your pattern at the center and side.

3. Square the center front/back and side of the pattern from full-hip level (or fullest measurement) to waist-seam level.

4. Measure and add together the width of the front and back at waist level between the squared lines drawn in step 3. Multiply by two for the total width. Subtract 2½ in. from the total width to account for seam allowances to determine the actual finished garment width. This measurement should be at least 2 in. larger than your largest measurement below your waist. If it isn't, redraw the line between the full hip and waist level, angling it so that the total waist measurement is at least 2 in. larger.

5. To form the casing, extend the line drawn in step 3 above the waistline. The extension amount will be two times the width of the elastic plus ¼ in. ease and a ⅝-in. seam allowance.

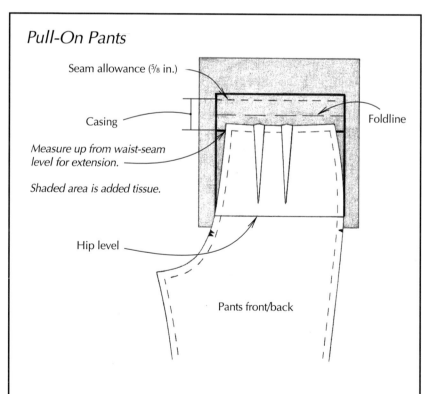

Pull-On Pants

Seam allowance (⅝ in.)

Casing

Measure up from waist-seam level for extension.

Shaded area is added tissue.

Hip level

Foldline

Pants front/back

Tape a large piece of see-through paper under the pattern from the hip to above the waist. Square a line from hip to waist level at the front, back, and side(s). Add an extension for the casing above the waist. The amount of the casing should equal two times the width of the elastic plus ¼ in. ease and one ⅝-in. seam allowance.

For example, for 1-in. elastic, the total extended amount will be 2⅞ in. The foldline will be halfway between the waistline and the seam allowance line.

The length of the elastic should equal the waist measurement minus 1½ in., or whatever is comfortable when the elastic is pulled around your waist, plus an allowance (1 in.) for overlap or joining of the elastic. Use a nonroll elastic in the desired width (¾ in. to 1½ in.).

Waist Finishes

There are several types of bands or finishes that may fit your particular shape better, be more comfortable, and be complementary to your fabric. This new finish will give your pants a different look, and you may prefer it to the band style that was included with your commercial pattern. In all instances, the construction sequence is the same, but how the waist finish is constructed and applied is different. If you have made a waist-size adjustment on your pattern or a fitting alteration, it may be easier to cut your waistband using your measurement rather than adjusting the pattern piece.

Considerations

Before designing your new waist finish, you need to do the following:
- Decide where the opening is going to be.
- Decide how much extension (over/underlap) you will need. Front and side closures lap right over left; back closures lap left over right.
- Consider applying preshrunk tape to the waistline to prevent stretching. It should be the length of the waistline seam, without seam allowances, from opening edge to opening edge. It is applied at the same time the waist sewn to the pants.
- Determine the finished width.
- Select an appropriate interfacing for reinforcement and stabilization, except for a fully elasticized band.

Faced finish

A waist facing is an exact copy (without darts) of the edge it is intended to finish. This type of finish is good for rectangular figures, where there is little or no waist definition. It also gives a more pleasing proportion to figures with long legs.

A faced waistline provides a smooth, clean finish that does not extend above the waistline. The facing, which is attached to the right side of the garment and ends up on the wrong side, is usually made from self fabric. If the fashion fabric is heavy or bulky, it can be made from a lighter-weight fabric.

The patternmaking procedure for this type of finish—replacing a separate straight fitted waistband—is the same as for a raised waist (see p. 139), except the facing extends from the waist down 2½ in. Use reinforcing tape in the waistline. If lining the pants, baste the lining to the pants at the waist seam before applying the facing.

Ribbon Facing

If being comfortable as well as fashionable is your goal, make your waistband narrower or face the waist edge with ribbon to eliminate the tight, bound-in feeling a fitted waistband can cause. A ribbon finish has the look of a faced finish from the outside, but the raw edge of the pants waist is finished with a firm ribbon such as ½-in. or ¾-in. preshrunk grosgrain or precontoured Petersham (available in white or black). The length of the grosgrain or Petersham should be your waist measurement plus 1¼ in.

If lining your pants, baste the lining to the pants-waist seam before applying the ribbon. No taping is required since the ribbon acts as a stabilizer. Trim ½ in. from the garment waist seam allowance, leaving ⅛ in.

Match and pin the edge of the ribbon or Petersham to the fabric edge of the pants waist. Stitch using a ⅛-in. seam allowance and easing the pants to fit. Turn the ribbon to the inside of the pants and tack to the seam allowances at the seams. Wrap ⅝ in. of the ribbon to the wrong side at the zipper opening and tack in place.

Fitted-contour waistband

This is a separate fitted band that sits above the waist, much like a traditional straight waistband. However, the band is slightly curved. The edge joining the pants is longer than the upper edge, "contouring" better to the shape of the body. This type of band is good if you have a sway back or a small waist in relation to your high hip or buttocks. If the top of your waistbands tend to stand away from your body, try this version. The waistband works with a center-front closing, or it can be adapted for a side closure. For the example that follows and is shown in the drawing on the facing page, the finished width will be 1¼ in., which is the standard width of a straight band.

1. On a piece of paper draw a rectangle. The width should be 1¼ in. The length should be equal to your waist measurement (column 1 on your Measurement Chart). Cut out the rectangle on the drawn lines.

Fitted-Contour Waistband

Step 1
Draw a rectangle. The width should equal 1¼ in., and the length should equal your waist measurement. Cut out the rectangle.

Steps 2 and 3
Divide the rectangle into quarters. Label them center front, side seam, center back, side seam, and center front.

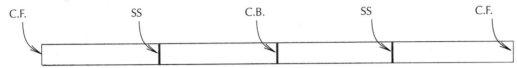

Step 4
To the left and right of center back, mark six equally spaced lines.

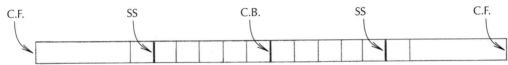

Steps 5 and 6
Cut on marked lines and spread ⅛ in. Tape in place.

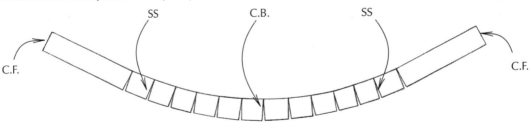

Steps 7 and 8
Add ⅝-in. seam allowance. Draw a line through center back for grain.

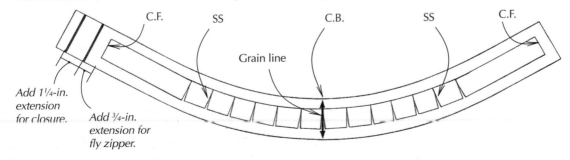

2. Fold the rectangle into quarters by first folding the length in half. Then fold the half in half again to create the quarters.

3. Mark the center back (the middle fold), side seams (the fold to each side of center back), and center front (the ends).

4. To the right and left of center back, mark six equally spaced lines. Four should be between center back and the side seam, one will be at the side seam, and the sixth will be positioned slightly past the side seam toward center front. The spacing between the lines should *look* reasonably balanced. The spaces do not have to be precise. The lines should extend the width of the rectangle.

5. Cut a piece of paper 12 in. wide by your waist measurement plus 4 in. For the following steps move to a firm surface that you can put pins into, such as an ironing board. Cut on the lines you have drawn on the rectangle, as well as on center back and the side-seam marks. Cut from one edge to the other, but *do not* separate the pieces.

Place the cut rectangle on the paper and place a pin at the center back edge, which is still attached, and into the working surface to hold in place. Spread the cut edge at center back 1/8 in.

and pin to hold the upper and lower edges. To determine how much to spread each additional cut line, I will use my own example.

My waist measures 27¼ in. Where I attach my band to my pants (the lower edge of my waist) I measure 28½ in. because I begin to curve out immediately below my waist. The difference is 1¼ in. When I wear a fitted straight waistband, it fits my pants but gaps at the top of the center back. I can pinch out a ⅝-in. fold. This is the amount I need to spread the cut edge.

Spread the measurement difference equally between the 12 other cuts and pin in place. The spreads are small, about ⅛ in. or less depending on your measured difference. If you are not sure how much to spread the cut edge, spread it so it is 1 in. larger than the upper measurement of the rectangle (the uncut edge). This measurement can be fine-tuned in subsequent pants.

6. Once you have the cuts spread evenly on both sides of center back to equal your larger measurement, tape in place.

7. Draw a line from edge to edge though the middle of the spread at center back. For fly zippers, measure the distance between the center front and the zipper teeth on the underlay side of the zipper (½ in. to ¾ in.). Add this amount to the left side of the contoured band. Add 1¼ in. to the right side for an extension closure.

8. Add seam allowances to all edges. Your fitted contour band is now completely customized to your measurements and body contour.

9. Cut two bands from fabric. One will be the outside band, the other the inside or facing. Lay center back on the straight grain. Cut interfacing from the same pattern and on the same grainline if using a woven fabric. One or both pieces can be interfaced depending on the firmness desired.

10. The upper, or narrower, edges of the two band pieces are sewn together. The seams are graded, clipped, and understitched. The lower edge is joined to the pants and completed in the same manner as for a straight-fitted waistband.

Partially elasticized waistband

Do you find your waistline fluctuating and your pants waistband a little too loose one day and too tight another? Help has arrived. This waistband has a smooth look in the front, with shirred elastic at the side back and a smooth center back. Follow these steps to modify your pattern.

1. Determine your largest and smallest comfortable waist measurement. Measure yourself at different times of the day, both sitting and standing, and on different days. Determine the difference between the largest and smallest measurements. For example, if your largest measurement is 32 in. and your smallest is 30 in., then the difference is 2 in. If you divide the difference by four, you will get the amount you should add to the side-seam waist on the front and back. For this example, that amount would be ½ in.

2. Add one-fourth of the total difference (as was just determined in step 1) at the side waist on the front and back pants pattern, tapering to "0" at your full hip depth (see the drawing on p. 148).

3. Measure the width of the side back dart at the waistline seam. The side back dart will be eliminated, but the take up (width between the legs at the waistline) will be added to the back side seam.

4. Cut the original waistband apart at the side seams. Increase each side front one-fourth of the total difference (½ in.). Increase the center-back waistband piece 1¼ in. on each side.

Pattern Development for Partially Elasticized (Side-Back) Waistband

Before you begin working on your pattern you'll need to determine the difference between the largest and smallest waist measurement.

Eliminate dart.

Steps 2 and 3 on back

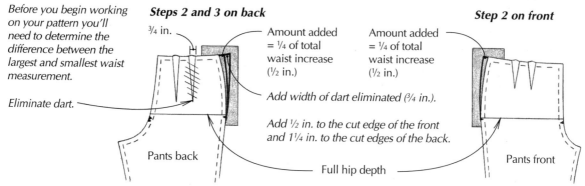

¾ in.

Amount added
= ¼ of total
waist increase
(½ in.)

Add width of dart eliminated (¾ in.).

Add ½ in. to the cut edge of the front and 1¼ in. to the cut edges of the back.

Pants back

Step 2 on front

Amount added
= ¼ of total
waist increase
(½ in.)

Full hip depth

Pants front

Step 4a

Cut the waistband apart at the side seams.

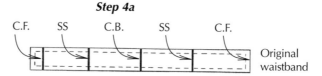

C.F.   SS   C.B.   SS   C.F.

Original
waistband

Step 4b

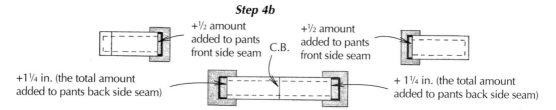

+½ amount
added to pants
front side seam

C.B.

+½ amount
added to pants
front side seam

+1¼ in. (the total amount
added to pants back side seam)

+ 1¼ in. (the total amount
added to pants back side seam)

Step 5

Add ⅝-in. seam allowances to cut edges of front and back.

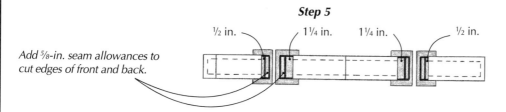

½ in.   1¼ in.   1¼ in.   ½ in.

Steps 6, 7 & 8

Measure 5 in. in from each back waistband seam allowance toward center back and mark the placement line for elastic. Stitch to the waistband. Join the waistband piece at side seams catching the elastic in the stitching.

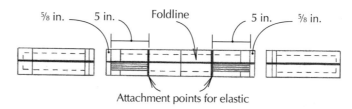

⅝ in.   5 in.   Foldline   5 in.   ⅝ in.

Attachment points for elastic

Step 9

Stretch the elastic flat while sewing parallel rows of stitching on the outside of the band.

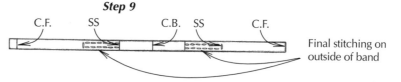

C.F.   SS   C.B.   SS   C.F.

Final stitching on
outside of band

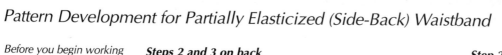

5. Add ⅝-in. seam allowances to each side front and each side of the center-back piece.

6. On the center-back piece, mark off 5 in. from the seam allowance toward center back on each side for the elastic placement.

7. The width of your elastic should be the same width as your finished band. Cut a 3½-in. length of Honeycomb or sport elastic (available in ¾-in. to 3-in. widths). This elastic looks like it has separate narrow channels of individual elastic, but it is actually one strip. It retains up to 90% of its stretch recovery when stitched through. Topstitching is done every ¼ in. to ½ in., depending on the width of your waistband. This elastic is especially comfortable at the side waist and looks great on a 2-in.-wide band.

8. Stitch a small amount (¼ in.) of elastic in with the side seam allowance when joining the waistband sections together and also at the point about 5 in. toward center back and perpendicular to the foldline (see the drawing on the facing page). **Note:** The elastic acts as an interfacing in the 5-in. area only. You will need to interface the remainder of the band as usual.

9. Attach the band as instructed in your guide sheet, matching side seams and stretching the back to fit. Finish the long edge of the facing side as desired or as instructed on your guide sheet. On the right side, evenly divide and mark the space between the fold and the garment seam into several parallel rows. Stretch the elastic flat while stitching through all waistband layers and elastic on marked lines.

Belt Loops

Decide how many belt loops you want. Four is the standard number, but an additional one at the center back will keep your belt from riding up. Sometimes belt loops are placed in pairs for a decorative effect. If you decide on pairs, make sure you multiply the number of pairs you want by two to get the right number of loops.

1. For a standard 1¼-in. finished waistband, begin with a 3-in.-long belt loop that is three times the desired finished width. For example, for four belt loops ⅜ in. wide, you will need a fabric strip 1⅛ in. wide and 12 in. long. Cut the strip with one long edge on the selvage, or serge one edge (see A in the drawing on p. 150).

2. Cut a ¼-in. strip of fusible web the length of the fabric strip.

Making Belt Loops

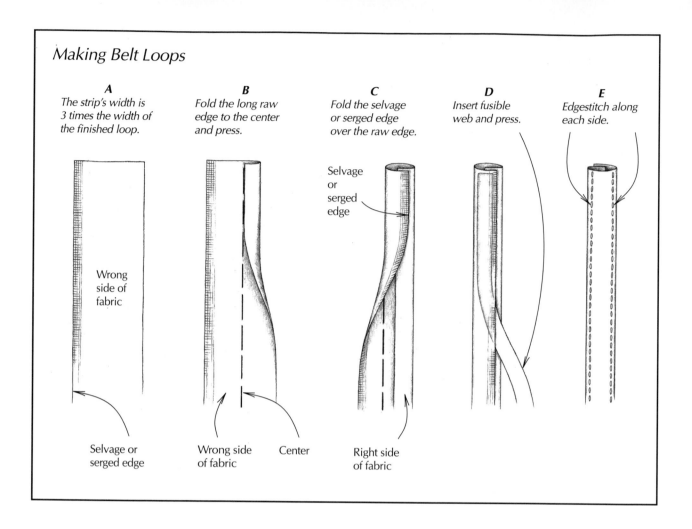

A
The strip's width is 3 times the width of the finished loop.

Wrong side of fabric

Selvage or serged edge

B
Fold the long raw edge to the center and press.

Wrong side of fabric   Center

C
Fold the selvage or serged edge over the raw edge.

Selvage or serged edge

Right side of fabric

D
Insert fusible web and press.

E
Edgestitch along each side.

3. Fold the fabric strip in half lengthwise and finger crease or lightly press it. (**B**)

4. Fold the long raw edge to center and press. (**B**)

5. Fold the selvage/serged edge over the raw edge and press. (**C**)

6. Tuck the narrow strip of fusible web under the long selvage/serged edge. Press to fuse in place. (**D**)

7. Edgestitch each long edge close to fold. (**E**)

Each finished belt loop will be 1¾ in. long with a ⅝-in. seam allowance at each end for attachment.

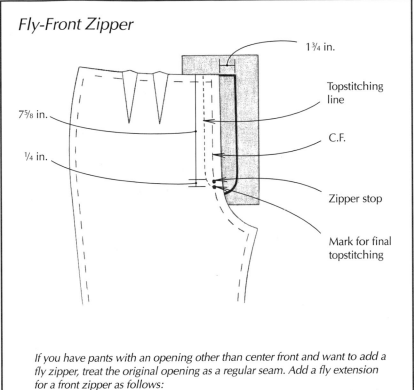

Fly-Front Zipper

1 ¾ in.

Topstitching line

C.F.

Zipper stop

Mark for final topstitching

7⅝ in.

¼ in.

If you have pants with an opening other than center front and want to add a fly zipper, treat the original opening as a regular seam. Add a fly extension for a front zipper as follows:
1. Mark the zipper stop 7⅝ in. down from the waist edge on center front.
2. Mark the start of the final topstitching line ¼ in. below the zipper stop.
3. Draw an extension that is 1¾ in. wide and parallel to center front from waist to topstitching mark.

Fly-Front Zipper

If you have pants with a zipper opening at the center back, you can add a fly-front zipper. Treat the original zipper opening as a regular seam, closing the entire seam when sewing it. To add a fly extension for a front zipper, make the following changes to your pattern, as shown in the drawing above:

1. On the pants center front, measure down 7⅝ in. from the waist edge and mark. This will be the zipper-stop mark.

2. Measure down ¼ in. from the zipper stop and mark. The final topstitching will begin at the lowest mark.

3. Draw a line parallel to center front and 1¾ in. from center front, even with the zipper stop. Draw a curved line to connect this parallel line to the mark ¼ in. below the zipper stop. This extension should be cut for both fronts.

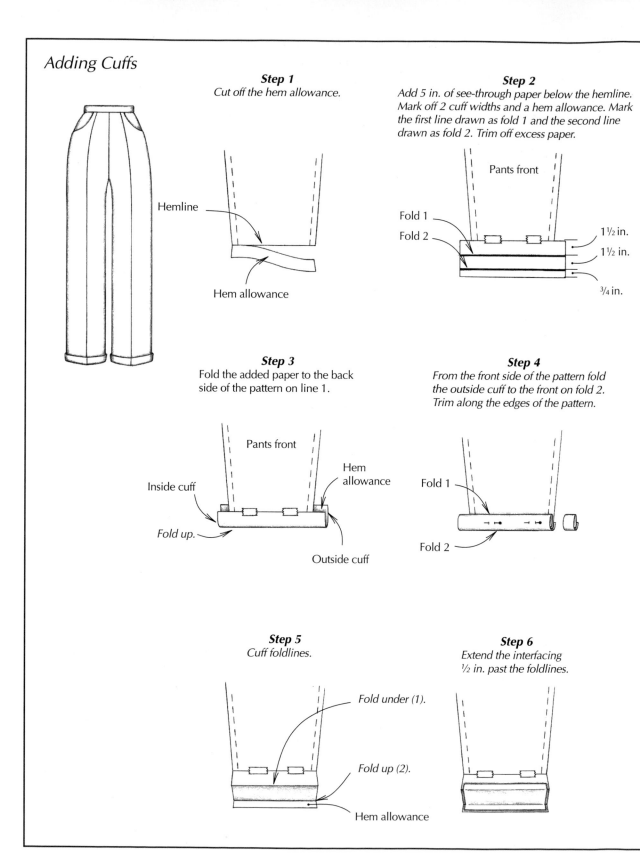

Adding Cuffs

Step 1
Cut off the hem allowance.

Hemline

Hem allowance

Step 2
Add 5 in. of see-through paper below the hemline. Mark off 2 cuff widths and a hem allowance. Mark the first line drawn as fold 1 and the second line drawn as fold 2. Trim off excess paper.

Pants front

Fold 1
Fold 2

1½ in.
1½ in.
¾ in.

Step 3
Fold the added paper to the back side of the pattern on line 1.

Pants front

Inside cuff

Fold up.

Hem allowance

Outside cuff

Step 4
From the front side of the pattern fold the outside cuff to the front on fold 2. Trim along the edges of the pattern.

Fold 1

Fold 2

Step 5
Cuff foldlines.

Fold under (1).

Fold up (2).

Hem allowance

Step 6
Extend the interfacing ½ in. past the foldlines.

Cuffs

Repeat steps 1 through 6 for front and back.

1. Draw in the hemline (the turn-up line for the hem) at the bottom of the pants front. Cut on the hemline, cutting off the hem allowance.

2. Decide on the finished width of the visible cuff (1½ in. is average). Widths vary with fashion. Tape a piece of paper 2 in. wider than the pants-leg width and about 5 in. long to the bottom of the pants leg. Add two cuff widths plus a ¾-in. hem allowance.

3. Crease on fold 1 (after the first cuff width), turning the outside cuff and hem allowance end up on the back side of the pattern.

4. From the front side of the pattern, crease at the bottom edge of the pattern (fold 2), folding up and bringing the remaining cuff on the back side to the front, leaving the hem allowance on the back side. Pin in place to hold. Trim the excess paper even with the pattern cutting line.

5. Unfold for the completed pattern.

6. Interface the cuffs with a fusible warp insertion interfacing or a bias strip of woven interfacing. Extend the interfacing ½ in. past the foldlines.

Tack the cuffs to the side and inner leg seams by machine or hand to hold in place.

Slant-Front Pockets with Optional Tummy Trim Panel

Once you have determined an accurate waistline fit for your pants and have perfected the side-seam hipline curve, you're ready to incorporate some design changes to transform the look of your pants using your original pattern.

One way is with slant-front pockets (see the drawing on pp. 156-157). The slant-front pocket continues to be popular because of its slenderizing effect on the figure. This classic pocket originates at the side hip. The opening is created by cutting away part of the pants front from the waist to the side seam. Traditionally these two points are connected with a diagonal style line on the front of the pants. The sack of this inserted pocket is hidden on the inside of the pants.

To preserve your original pattern as is and add a second pattern, simply make an exact tracing of the upper portion of your current pattern to a point 2 in. below the crotchline. This way you can interchange differently styled pants tops without having to retrace the whole leg portion.

1. If you are beginning with a pleated or darted pattern, fold the pattern pleat(s) or dart(s) closed as they would be when the garment is sewn (see step 1 in the drawing on pp. 156-157). Pin or tape them closed. If the darts or pleats are not closed when the pocket pattern is traced, they will be included in the pocket pattern, adding unnecessary bulk to the pocket when sewn.

2. Pin the pattern to your working surface. Place see-through paper over the pants front and secure it with removable tape or pins.

3. Plot and dot on the paper at the following points:
- waist and side intersection
- 4 in. from the side waist toward center front
- 2 in. from the side waist toward center front. This amount is a guideline. Plotting this point more than 2 in. will create a style line that is more horizontal. Plotting it less than 2 in. creates a more vertical pocket line. The more vertical the line, or parallel to the side seam, the more slimming the line.
- 6 in. to 7 in. from the waist along the side edge (for the pocket opening)
- 1 in. below the pocket opening marked above
- a horizontal line from the first dot on the side below the waist to center front

- a line from the waist dot closest to center front, parallel to the grainline, ending at crotch level. Plot a dot where these two lines intersect.
- Number the dots as shown in the drawing on pp. 156-157 (step 2).

4. From dot 4, measure down another 4 in. to 5 in. At this point draw a horizontal line halfway across the pants front, perpendicular to the grainline. This line should not be lower than the crotchline (step 2).

5. Connect dots 1 to 5, tracing the side edge of the pattern, then connect 5 to 6, making sure the deepest part of the pocket touches the lower horizontal line.

Hint: A French curve is helpful to get a smooth, well-shaped curve. Continue by connecting dot 6 to 2, 2 to 3, and 3 to 1, tracing the cutting edge of your pattern. Connect dot 3 to 4 in a straight or slightly curved line (step 3).

6. There will be two parts to the pocket (step 4):
- pocket underlay (dots 1-5-6-2-3-1)
- upper pocket/facing (dots 3-4-5-6-2-3)

The wedge pattern (dots 1-4-3-1) will be used to lay on the pants-front pattern, matching side and waist edges, to cut away that portion of the full front.

7. Make the notch markings on the pocket as indicated in step 5 to facilitate matching during construction. The grainline of the pocket is parallel to the pants grainline. Transfer single notch markings on the underlay side edge to the pants back side edge.

8. Lay see-through paper over the pattern and trace one upper pocket/facing and one wedge pattern. Remove all tracings and cut out one upper pocket/facing and one underlay and one wedge pattern (step 6).

9. Lay the wedge piece on the pants front, matching side and waist edges. Transfer the single notch marking on the angled edge of the wedge to the pants front. Cut off that portion of the pants-front pattern between dots 3 and 4 (step 8). Add a seam allowance to this edge (step 9).

10. About midway on the upper pocket/facing style edge, cut across to the opposite edge but do not separate the pieces. Place paper under the cut and spread the edge (between dots 3 and 4) about ¼ in. This will allow some ease in the pocket so it will fit better over the curve of the body and make it easier to use. Slightly more or less ease may be necessary because of the bulk of the fabric or your body shape. Redraw the style line between dots 3 and 4 and the grainline.

Add a seam allowance to style edge (between dots 3 and 4) (step 10).

11. The upper-pocket portion of the pocket can be cut from fashion fabric, pocketing, or lining since it will not be seen. If the upper pocket is cut from fabric other than fashion fabric, a fashion-fabric facing can be applied from the style edge 2 in. in, on top of the upper-pocket fabric to reduce bulk. The underlay can also be faced. The exact shape is not important as long as the pocketing fabric is well hidden and is not visible when worn or used. Finish the facing edges that extend into the pocket with a zigzag, clean finish, or serged edge before joining it to the pocket.

12. To add a tummy-trim panel, extend the pocket underlay to the front edge of the pattern. The extension length should be about 4¾ in. from the top waist edge (more if you lengthened the crotch depth, less if you shortened it) and should get caught in the center-front seam. This extension can be cut out of any lightweight fabric, stable tricot, power net, or even control-top panty hose (without the elastic band) and zigzagged to the pocket underlay. This will help the pleats lie flatter and prevent spreading if your pattern has been properly fitted (step 11).

Pattern Development for Slant-Front Pockets

Step 1

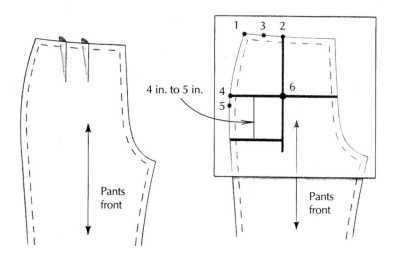

Pants
front

Steps 2, 3 & 4

4 in. to 5 in.

Pants
front

Step 5

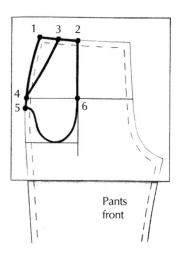

Pants
front

Step 6

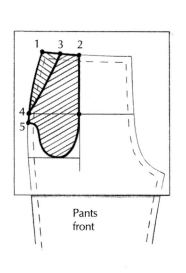

Pants
front

Step 7

Notches

Pants
front

Step 8

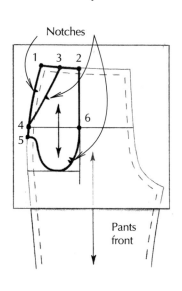

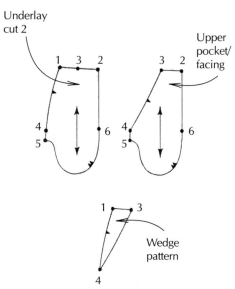

Underlay
cut 2

Upper
pocket/
facing

Wedge
pattern

 = 1-4-3-1 wedge to be cut away from full-front pattern   = 3-4-5-6-2-3 upper pocket/facing

Step 9a

Seam allowance

Pants
front

Step 9b

Seam allowance

Pants
front

Step 10

Slash

3

4
5

Seam
allowance

Cut 2.

Step 11—pattern for fashion fabric facings

Upper pocket

2 in.

Fashion
fabric

Underlay

3 in.

Fashion
fabric

Edge finish
needed

Step 12—tummy-trim panel

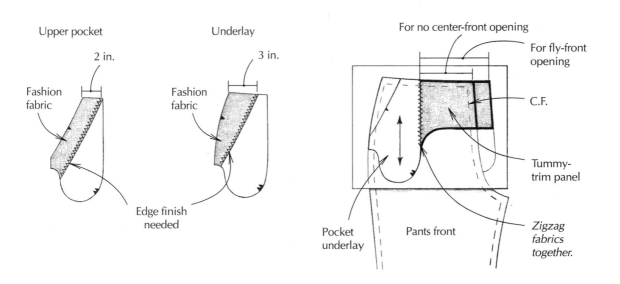

For no center-front opening

For fly-front
opening

C.F.

Tummy-
trim panel

Zigzag
fabrics
together.

Pocket
underlay

Pants front

Index

A

Acrylic, qualities of, 26

B

Basting, method for, 97
Belt loops:
  making, 149–50
  number of, 149
Boning, for raised waists, 140

C

Challis, qualities of, 26
Chino, qualities of, 26
Cleaning:
  detergents for, pH-balanced, 31
  by washing, 31
Closures:
  attaching, 123–24
  buttonhole, 123, 124
  choosing, 123
Construction. See also Cutting; Layout;
      Marking; Seams
  of lining, 92
  sequence for, 92
Corduroy, qualities of, 26
Cotton:
  qualities of, 25
  washing, 31
Creaselines, establishing, 100–101, 126
Crepe de Chine, qualities of, 26
Cuffs, adding, 152–53
Cutting:
      method for, 95
      of notches, 96

D

Darts. See also Flare; Gathers; Pleats
  basic, transforming, 130–36
  for buttocks, 87
  and excess fabric, 88
  for high hips, 87
  length of, altering, 88
  in linings, 98
  making, 101–102, 103
  marking, 101
  in measurements, 53
  for raised waists, 140
  reangling, 87
  reshaping, 88
  for sway back, 88
  tuck, 130
  working with, 85, 86
Denim, qualities of, 26

E

Ease, types of, defined, 15

F

Fabric:
  blends of, 26
    thread for, 29
  calculating, 30–31
  choosing, 22
  hand of, defined, 26–27
  for interfacing, 28–29
  for linings, 27–28
  natural, thread for, 29–30
  natural vs. manmade, 24–26
  needles for, 30
  pocketing, 28
  preshrinking, 31–32
  sewing-ready, 92
  synthetic, thread for, 29
  truing, 32–33
  yardage of, calculating, 30–31
Facings:
  for raised waists, 140–41
  for waistbands, 143–44
Figures:
  silhouettes of, charted, 18–20
  variations in, charted, 46
Fit. See also Jeans; Slacks; Trousers
  above crotch, 136
  analysis of, 80–81
  and crotch, 135, 136
  and crotch curve, 85, 86
  and crotch depth, 84, 85
  during construction, hints for, 93–94
  of hips, 83, 84–85, 86
  for leg back, 86
  sewing for, preliminary, 82
  of thighs, 83, 84–85
  with trial garment, 76
  of waist, 83, 84–85
  of waistbands, 119
Flare, from darts, 133–36
French tacks, illustrated, 127

G

Gabardine, qualities of, 26, 27
Gathers, darts into, 130–31

H

Hand, defined, 26–27
Hems:
  allowance for, altering, 136, 138
  cuffs with, adding, 152–53
  for flared pants, 133, 134
  sequence for, 125–26

I

Interfacing:
  boning for, 140
  marking for, 97
  material for, 28–29
  for raised waists, 140
  for waistbands, 119, 121
  for zippers, 107, 108, 112–13

J

Jeans, fit of, described, 10–11

K

Knits:
  qualities of, 26
  thread for, 29
  truing, 33

L

Layout, method for, 94–95
Leg styles:
  altering, 135–36
  flared, creating, 133–36
  lengths of,
    named, chart of, 137
    varying, 138–39
  narrow, measuring for, 134
  types of, 20, 134–35
  widths of, 16–17
Linen:
  qualities of, 25, 26
  washing, 31
Linings:
  advantages of, 27
  darts and pleats in, 98
  fabric for, 27–28
  French tacks for, 127
  layout for, 98
  for pockets, 28
  zippers and, 114–18

M

Marking:
  method for, 97
  tools for, 96–97
Measurements. See also Patterns
  chart for, 38
  crotch depth, 38, 39, 41, 42, 43
  crotch length, 38, 39, 44
  customizing, 36, 39
  full-hip, 38, 39, 40–41, 43, 45
  high-hip, 38, 39–40, 43
  knee, 41
  reference points for, 37, 39

thigh, 38, 39, 41, 43–44
waist, 38–40, 43
waist-to-floor, 38, 39, 42, 43
waist-to-knee, 38, 39, 43

N

Notions:
buying, 29
defined, 16, 29
Nylon, qualities of, 26

P

Patterns. See also Fit
adjusting, body-measurement chart
for, 38
adjustments to, colored pens for, 82
basic,
advantages of, 13–14
choosing, 14–15
buttocks in,
flat, adjustment for, 63, 64–65
high, adjustment for, 64, 65
protruding, adjustment for, 61–63
calves in, hyperextended, 71
chart for, increment, 52
copying, 47, 153
crotch depth of, adjusting, 48–51
crotch-length of, adjustments for, 71–72
crotchline on, 48, 49
ease in, 44, 45
final fit on, 88–89
full-hip in, adjustment for, 51, 53,
57–58, 67, 84
one, adjustment for, 65–66
high-hip in, adjustment for, 56, 84
knees in,
bowed, adjustment for, 69, 70–71
knock, adjustment for, 67–68
line for, 48, 49
measurement of, 135
lengths of, marking, 47
multisized, adjusting, 47
paper for, 54, 73, 89
reading, 16
recopying, 89
reference points of, 49
refinements in, 58–59
seam allowances in, 45–46, 47
adding, 77
testing, 75–77
thighs in,
adjustment for, 51, 53, 54, 58–60, 84
full-front, adjustment for, 59, 60
full-inner, adjustment for, 60
truing, 73–75
tummy in, protruding, adjustment for,
60–61

waistband in, adjusting, 54–56
waist in, adjusting, 53, 54–56
waist-to-floor in, adjusting, 51
waist-to-knee in, adjusting, 51
Pleats:
darts into, 131–33
in linings, 98
in measurements, 53
making, 102, 103
marking, 102
working with, 86
Pockets, cutting, 102
inseam, 103–104
interfacing for, 102
linings for, 28
making, 102–105
options for, 21
side-opening, 105
slant-front, adding, 153–56
Polyester, qualities of, 26
Pressing:
of darts, 102
techniques for, 99
tools for, 98–99
Pull-on pants. See Waists: elasticized,
gathered

R

Rayon:
qualities of, 25
washing, 31

S

Seams:
allowances for,
adding, 77
in linings, 98
in patterns, 45–46, 47
crotch, 114, 116
finishes of, 100
plain, 100
Sewing. See Construction; Seams
Sewing machines:
needle sizes for, 30
stitch lengths of, 30
Shorts, from pants patterns, 138–39
Silk:
jersey, qualities of, 26
pongee, qualities of, 26
qualities of, 25
washing, 31
Slacks, fit of, described, 11–12
Spandex, qualities of, 26
Styles:
and figure types, 18–20
sketches of, 20

T

Tape, basting, double-sided, 29
Thread:
choices in, 28, 29–30
polyester, 29
Trousers, fit of, described, 11–12
Tummy-trim panels, adding, 155, 157

U

Ultrasuede, qualities of, 26

W

Waistbands. See also Belt loops
closures for, 123
facings for, 120
fitting, 54–56, 118–119
pre-, 119
over pleats, 133
sewing, 119–23
and zippers, 120
Waists:
elasticized,
gathered, 141–43
partially, 147–49
faced, 21, 143–44
fitted, 21
contour, 144–47
gathered, 21
interfacing for, 140
raised, 139
ribbon finish for, 144
Wool:
crepe, qualities of, 26
jersey, qualities of, 26
preshrinking, 31–32
qualities of, 25

Z

Zippers:
center-back, to fly-front, 150–51
choices in, 28
fly, 107–108
interfacing, 107, 108–10, 112–13
invisible, 111–13
and linings, 114–18
pinless centered, 106–107
polyester, 29
preshrinking, 106
shortening, 105, 106
topstitching, 110
and waistbands, 120

Look for these and other *Threads* books at your local bookstore or sewing retailer.

Easy Guide to Serging Fine Fabrics	*Beyond the Pattern*
Easy Guide to Sewing Blouses	*Distinctive Details*
Easy Guide to Sewing Jackets	*Fit and Fabric*
Easy Guide to Sewing Linings	*Fitting Solutions*
Easy Guide to Sewing Skirts	*Fitting Your Figure*
Just Pockets	*Great Quilting Techniques*
Sew the New Fleece	*Great Sewn Clothes*
The Sewing Machine Guide	*Jackets, Coats and Suits*
Fine Machine Sewing	*Quilts and Quilting*
50 Heirloom Buttons to Make	*Sewing Tips & Trade Secrets*
Couture Sewing Techniques	*Stitchery and Needle Lace*
Shirtmaking	*Techniques for Casual Clothes*

For a catalog of the complete line of *Threads* books and videos, write to The Taunton Press, Inc., P.O. Box 5506, Newtown, CT 06470-5506.